MW00694854

My Time with
GENERAL
COLIN POWELL

Published by Lisa Hagan Books 2023

www.lisahaganbooks.com

Copyright © Leslie Lautenslager 2023

ISBN: 978-1-945962-58-5

All Rights Reserved. No part of this publication may be reproduced, stored in a retrieval system, or transmitted in any form, or by any means, electronic, mechanical, photocopying, recording or otherwise without the prior permission in writing of the copyright holders, nor be otherwise circulated in any form or binding or cover other than in which it is published and without a similar condition being imposed on the subsequent publisher.

Cover and interior layout by Simon Hartshorne

My Time with
GENERAL
COLIN POWELL

Stories of Kindness, Diplomacy, & Protocol

LESLIE LAUTENSLAGER
with Bradley Harper

Testimonials

"Leslie Lautenslager was my father's indispensable aide for decades, but she was also a valued member of our family. She has written an intimate portrait of a man who had many sides that few people got to see. Our family is grateful to Leslie for capturing the richness of our beloved patriarch."
—The Honorable Michael Powell, Colin Powell's Son

"Colin Powell was a fiercely loyal person, and I can hardly remember a time when Leslie wasn't a reliable fixture in our family. She was there for us as much as she was for her General. Leslie actually put her formidable event and protocol skills to work on my wedding and also got us through the very difficult days and weeks after we lost him. When she started working for my dad, I was in my 20s and off on my own personal journey. Like any offspring in that phase of life, I was selfishly paying very little attention to what my parents were up to. Now as a fully formed adult, this book by my "sister from another mister" is a tremendous gift. It is a window into parts of my sweet daddy's life to which I had no access, and which will help keep his memory alive for me and my children."
—Ann Powell, Colin Powell's Daughter

"Dearest Leslie--This is so exciting and my warmest congratulations. I am so proud of you."

—Love, Lucky

(Lucky is Ambassador Selwa Roosevelt, the U.S. Chief of Protocol under President Ronald Reagan)

"When I met Ms. Leslie Lautenslager in 2017, she was the President of Protocol & Diplomacy International--Protocol Officers Association. Later on, we had some academic interaction. In 2018, I invited her to contribute a paper to the book that I edited named, *A Study of Diplomatic Protocol and Etiquette: From Theory to Practice.* She generously accepted the invitation and contributed a wonderful paper. In my eyes, she is a lady with a charming personality which is elegant, considerate, and thoughtful. Leslie served as special assistant to former Secretary of State General Colin Powell for over 25 years and was one of the people who knew him best. Now Leslie's book *MY TIME WITH GENERAL COLIN POWELL: STORIES OF KINDNESS, DIPLOMACY & PROTOCOL* is being published. For those who wish to learn about General Powell, diplomacy and protocol, I believe this will be a rare good book."

—Jiali Zhou, Associate Professor, China Foreign Affairs University

Contents

DEDICATIONS

In honor of
my mother Margaret Duke Lautenslager
and
my brother Edwin "Win" Lautenslager
In memory of
my father Edwin "Jack" Lautenslager
and
my General Colin Powell

General Powell's faxed welcome note that
presaged his dreaded "love notes."

PREFACE

On the speaking circuit, I often found my client contacts to be intimidated by the prospect of meeting and working with General Powell. After developing a bit of a rapport over the phone, I'd dramatically sigh and tell them all the good things they had ever heard about the General were wrong. In the stunned silence that followed, I would respond sotto voce, "He's even better!"

The historians and analysts will write—and have written—books and articles about General Powell's legacy and place in history. The world saw him as a military leader, a diplomat, a senior statesman, and an advocate for young people. To friends and family, he was so much more: he was funny and charming, self-deprecating, and practical; generous, gracious, and kind. He was also a song and dance man, a car aficionado, a handyman, a lover of comfort food, a standup comedian, and a storyteller. I can't keep from smiling when I think of that Colin Powell, the man behind the public persona.

General Powell was also blessed with a fabulous family. I adore Mrs. Powell, their children and in-laws (Michael and Jane, Linda, Annemarie and Francis), their grandchildren, and their extended family—both those related by blood and those not. No matter how close I have been to the family over the years though, this book does not include their stories. I did my best to protect their privacy through the years of working with the General and will continue to do so. Without a doubt though, I delight in being a part of that extended not-by-blood family and relish every time Michael calls me "Sis."

The chapters that follow are not in chronological order. This is not meant to be a historical memoir. Instead, I share a multitude of stories, lessons, and laughs I experienced with General Powell during more than a quarter century at his side. Each chapter is thematic and can stand alone. To give credit where credit is due, this is the same pattern General Powell followed in his book, *It Worked For Me: In Life and Leadership.* I have included quotes of his throughout the chapters in hopes of sharing his voice.

In finishing this book, I have come to realize that, in addition to being a tribute to my beloved General, this is also a love letter to all the assistants, aide-de-camps, protocol professionals, event planners, and managers who work tirelessly behind the scenes and beside the officials who make the headlines.

Without question, I know I was incredibly fortunate to work with, learn from, and have the admiration, support, and love of a truly remarkable and one-of-a-kind individual. I only wish everyone could be so lucky and blessed.

1.

Beside My General

"Have a vision. Be demanding."
　—Colin Powell

I'm the perfect example of the person who was in the right place at the right time. I had no plan, no grand design. My journey of over a quarter of a century with General Colin Powell began with a gentle nudge from fate.

To begin, let me describe something that happened several weeks prior to meeting the man I grew to love and whom I would accompany around the world.

The closest I ever came to being a lady-in-waiting was in April 1996 when I assisted my former boss, Ambassador Selwa "Lucky" Roosevelt, with the annual Washington National Opera Gala. Each WNO Gala is a prestigious black-tie event attended by the most powerful people within government and private industry—the who's who from Washington and around the world. Besides handwriting the calligraphy for the dinner place cards and helping with the seating for the after-performance dinner, I staffed Ambassador Roosevelt, the Chairman of the Gala. "Staffing" a principal means you are the go-to person the dignitary relies upon.

This can require a variety of tasks—anything from "carrying the football" or being the "body man" for the President, to providing the introductions for receiving lines. That night I was the designated guardian angel for Ambassador Roosevelt amidst the glitterati.

Her exquisite gown had a train, so among my more complicated duties I had to keep it from being tripped over as we progressed regally up the stairs of the Kennedy Center Opera House for the VIP champagne reception. As I was defending Ambassador Roosevelt's train, while not stumbling myself in my heels and floor-length gown, I recognized Alma Powell just ahead of us. Although her husband was beside her, I only had eyes for Mrs. Powell, thinking of how much I hoped to meet her someday. Everyone else wanted to mingle with the General, but I wanted to meet Mrs. Powell as she exuded elegance, grace, and charm—qualities I admire tremendously.

I didn't meet Mrs. Powell that night, but the gala was spectacular and life as I knew it went on.

A couple weeks later I received a phone call from Pam Ahearn, a dear friend and former Office of Protocol colleague, saying her husband had just left a message: *"How fast can you find Leslie? I've just learned of a job with her name on it and they need her immediately."*

The job was with the Washington Speakers Bureau (WSB) working as an event coordinator for one of the most popular speakers on the lecture circuit: General Colin L. Powell, USA (Ret.). General Powell had already finished a wildly successful book tour for his first book, *My American Journey*, and was in high demand. When the WSB event coordinator who had served him announced she was leaving the company, co-founders Bernie Swain and Harry Rhoads told the General—their golden goose at the time—that they would hire whomever he wanted for the position.

I will be forever grateful General Powell replied that, since they had taken good care of him up till then, he trusted them to find the right replacement.

Bernie and Harry then scoured their network throughout the public speaking world; it was just plain good luck that they inquired with my friend's husband, Rick Ahearn, who was chief of staff to former Senator Jack Kemp, another popular speaker. Although I did not come from the military, Rick believed I was right for the job based on my protocol background and, like the General, I had worked in the Reagan administration.

Within two days of the call, I interviewed with Bernie Swain and was offered the job on the spot. Although I was very impressed, I'd always heard one should never accept a job immediately, so I said I'd think it over and let him know by the end of the week. I needed to give the job careful consideration and not be swayed prematurely by Bernie's offer, no matter how appealing. I didn't know it at the time, but I was following one of General Powell's thirteen rules, "You can't make someone else's choices. You shouldn't let someone else make yours."

However, when I said I'd think it over, Bernie looked like I'd just stolen his puppy. Seeing his reaction, I asked if I could at least sleep on it and let him know in the morning, and he agreed.

Bernie played to win, so when I got home that evening, two dozen beautiful long-stemmed roses awaited with a note that said simply, "*Hope you will join us. Bernie and Harry.*"

I was already pretty sure what my decision would be, but that lovely gesture sealed the deal, and first thing the next morning, I called and said yes.

I had not yet met General Powell, so I was scheduled to visit his office within the next week or so. I had taken the job assuming

I wouldn't actually work much with him directly but through his staff, as surely he was surrounded by an entourage and an extensive bureaucracy. Having grown up in the Washington, D.C. area, I was accustomed to the powerful surrounding themselves with layers of support staff ("straphangers," to use a common military and government term). In General Powell's case, I could not have been more wrong.

There is a condition known as White Coat Syndrome, which describes how certain people's blood pressure elevates when they see a doctor. I suspect I had the military equivalent—call it a Fatigues Syndrome or a Dress Blues Syndrome maybe. Not coming from a military background, I found being with someone who had held the top military position in the U.S. military (if not in all the militaries of the entire world) intimidating. Although General Powell had been retired a few years by now, in my mind his four stars still sparkled blindingly on his shoulders even on his civilian attire.

When I arrived for the first meeting, he welcomed me into his small office in Old Town Alexandria, just a few blocks from the Washington Speakers Bureau. I had already been greeted warmly by his staff of four, including Bill Smullen and Peggy Cifrino, his fiercely loyal and tremendously talented Chief and Deputy Chief of Staff, but now it was time to sit down alone with *the* General himself.

Later, General Powell and I often laughed about our first impressions of each other. He swore he was warm and encouraging, but to me he was towering and intimidating. I'm certain I was nervous and uncomfortable; he described me as serene and calm. We also argued laughing that although I believed it took me a full year to shed my intimidation, he believed it only took a month. He might have been right.

In our final couple of years together, General Powell often teased me that I should write a book. My response was always that I would write a book on protocol someday, as I had done quite a bit of writing on that topic already and had previously even been published in China. Every time I said this, he would roll his eyes, exaggerate a yawn, and say with a laugh, "But you gotta write about me! You want it to sell, don't you?"

Time can heal heartache and provide a new perspective. My grief after his death has been overtaken by an overwhelming need to share *my* General with the world, to share his funny and inspiring stories, his innumerable acts of kindness and diplomacy, and yes, even stories about protocol (if for no other reason than to explain why I was in the room). Historians and pundits will continue to write about General Powell's accomplishments as a military leader and diplomat. They will debate his decisions and place in history while extoling the example he set for young people and succeeding generations. That's all fine, but let this, my effort, be a portrait of the person behind the public eye and headlines. Let me share the wonderful man he was, and the man I knew. I am gripped by the feeling that not to do so would be unforgivably selfish.

I end this chapter as it began, by mentioning former U.S. Chief of Protocol Ambassador Selwa "Lucky" Roosevelt. I was visiting at her home a few months before General Powell died and we were reminiscing about my early days of protocol in the 1980s, when she welcomed me onto her staff at the State Department. Under her wing, I was introduced to the art and science of protocol. She taught me that the formal etiquette of diplomacy sets the stage for nurturing mutual respect between countries, cultures, and leaders. Our lives of service make the world a better place.

That vision and knowledge became the foundation of my career serving General Powell.

As we shared memories, Ambassador Roosevelt used the French phrase "*joie de vivre*" to describe our shared remembrances.

Joie de vivre: an exuberant enjoyment of life.

That is exactly how I would describe my many years working with General Colin L. Powell, USA (Ret.). Working with, for, and beside him was an exuberantly joyful time.

Now, let me share him.

2.

From Scratch

*"The troops may whine and moan, but when they meet
the standard, there's a sense of pride."*
—Colin Powell

In 1996 email was not a thing, or at least not at the Washington Speakers Bureau (WSB). When I started staffing General Powell on the speaking circuit, we communicated by phone, fax, or in person.

On one of my first days at WSB, I was away from my desk when I heard the receptionist announce my name over the loudspeaker, saying the General was on the line. Waiting. For me. I think I'm usually pretty calm under pressure, but at that moment I was more like a Looney Tunes cartoon character as the papers in my hands flew skyward and I spun on my heels and rushed back to my desk. What he needed turned out to be simple and easily resolved, but out of breath, I almost stood at attention and saluted.

In both of General Powell's books—his autobiography, *My American Journey*, and his book on leadership, *It Worked For Me: In Life and Leadership*—he described in great detail how he trained his new aides and assistants. Unfortunately, I had not yet read his autobiography, and he had yet to write his other book.

Consequently, those first few weeks were painful, and I frankly did not like him much as I learned his unique management style.

Like any young professional, I believed I had strong initiative and was adept at problem solving. I was also exceptionally good at following instructions. I would start each day happy to walk into my little corner of the office to embrace whatever tasks awaited me.

But only until I would find a note waiting for me on the fax machine, stating:

TO: LL

FROM: CP

RE: LOVE NOTE

Oh, how I dreaded those "love notes."

Each note would contain a long litany of what I had done wrong the previous day, and clear instructions on what to do (and not do) in the future. The worst part about these "love notes" was they were typed entirely in ALL CAPS. Apparently, no one had ever taught General Powell that typing in all caps is the equivalent of shouting.

I eventually learned to take them, if not in stride, then at least as the teaching tools he intended. While he was forming me into the aide-de-camp he needed, I slowly realized I had some influence on him, too, and finally I broke him of his all-caps habit.

In later years, during many of his Zoomed discussions on leadership, General Powell would regale executives with his "love note" technique of training staff and for comic relief would often pull me over to join him on the computer screen in order to describe my reaction. We always got the laughs we intended before sharing the lesson learned. Any leader will be more effective in nurturing new "recruits" if expectations are outlined early, directly, and explicitly, explaining both the minute details and the big picture needed for success. As the General often said, "If you are going to achieve excellence in big things, you develop the habit in little matters."

*   *   *

General Powell's post-retirement career revolved around his commitment to boards, philanthropic work, and the international speaking circuit. After leaving the State Department, he accepted invitations from Marc Benioff of Salesforce and KR Sridhar of Bloom Energy to join their respective boards. As both companies are based in California, their director meetings required trips to the West Coast several times a year. In addition, he was devoted to his alma mater, the City College of New York, and to its school named after him, The Colin Powell School for Civic and Global Leadership. The General's dedication to these responsibilities and his paid speaking engagements were the anchors on his calendar around which the rest of his obligations were planned.

Part of my job was to minimize his time on the road and keep the "calendar footprint" as small as possible. He always preferred to fly in or drive to the engagement, arrive on site, glad hand (or as he would say, "make his manners"), do the gig, and return home immediately after. That ideal was rarely entirely possible, but he made it clear that part of my mission was to get him back home quickly. I can still hear his voice saying, "There is no hotel, restaurant, museum, nor shopping in the world that would appeal to me more than being in my own backyard in McLean. Your job is to get me back home to Alma as soon as you possibly can."

This job was achieved in part by maintaining a certain level of privacy at all times. When the sales agents at WSB wanted to check the General's availability for a speaking engagement, they knew to ask me to check what I had dubbed the "Secret Squirrel Calendar," the personal Powell calendar I kept that was not shared publicly. During the four years I was at the State Department with him, one of the phone lines on my desk was what my staff jokingly referred to as "the Bat Phone." The only one who had that number was the Secretary of State, i.e., my General. My colleagues knew to never answer it in my absence. Whenever I returned to the office, all they had to say was that a call had come in on the bat line and I knew the Secretary needed me.

General Powell only allowed those closest to him to know the private number that would go directly to him without first being screened by layers of assistants. Although I rarely used it, just knowing I was one of those who could have was tremendously affirming.

Over the years, I quickly learned that if he answered the phone with "*Whattaya say?*" it was a rhetorical question. It also meant he had too much time on his hands in his home office, "the Bunker," and he was ready to review the "honey-do" list.

I knew the only time I was in trouble with the boss was if he began a call with a stern, "*Leslie, this is General Powell,*" as if I could not recognize his voice immediately. Fortunately, I think he only ever identified each of us by name on the phone like this twice in all our many years together.

No matter how much I begrudged his early training, which was like drinking from a fire hose, a quarter century later I'll admit those painful lessons became ingrained and served us both well.

*　*　*

His touchstone instruction when preparing for any event was his oft-stated words, "Make me smart." He was a good teacher, but also a good student, and never stopped doing his homework. I often surprised contacts within an organization planning a speaking engagement by asking for the company's annual reports, details about participants and board members, industry trends, and other minutiae seemingly unrelated to the event. When they responded that surely General Powell would have no interest in reading these details, since other speakers never did, I would answer that not only did he read them all, but he would do his own digging to find out even more. Then I'd explain, in case it wasn't already obvious, that he was not like other speakers.

On the speaking circuit, he never used a written speech and rarely even referred to notes while on stage. All his advance preparation allowed him to surprise the audience with his detailed knowledge about all aspects of the organization, the industry, and the event. Attendees were always wowed by his performance, and knowing the details was his gift to his hosts.

Ah, to see that Cheshire Cat grin spread across his face when he sensed an audience was blown away by his seeming clairvoyance—it was impossible not to find his joy infectious.

I'm not sure if it was from his military training or simply because his mother raised him right, but General Powell was a strong proponent for writing thank-you notes. It was his practice after an event to immediately pen a handwritten note of thanks to the head of the company who'd hosted him. Over the years, I lost count of how many times I would hear from my contact that the leadership had rarely, if ever, received a thank you from a speaker before.

* * *

Whatever my official title to General Powell was under the umbrella of the Washington Speakers Bureau, and later at the Department of State, I was an aide-de-camp for him. I know neither of us ever imagined that from those early days we would fall into step together so naturally.

Early on, when I was still a bit intimidated and before I started traveling with him, we did not carry cell phones and were still years away from texting. Every time I arranged the car service to take General Powell from his home to the airport, I would call his driver's car phone within a few moments of the General's scheduled arrival. Part of this was to calm a paranoia that I hadn't scheduled the car correctly, but it was also to assure myself that the General was in the car and no longer my worry. This pattern went on seamlessly (so I thought) for a few weeks and I was relieved I'd established a perfect plan for double-checking my logistics.

This was true until one evening when Page Parvez, his long-time local car service driver, answered my call then told me to hold on. Within seconds, General Powell picked up the phone and laughingly said, "*All this time I've been wondering how Page's phone somehow always rings within minutes of my getting in the car. I finally figured out it had to be you.*"

Thus, was born our tradition that every time he got into a car whether he was on my watch or not we touched base with each other. It was a reassurance to make sure we were where we needed to be, and all was right with our world.

It wasn't easy to avoid stressing out over managing someone so well-known and revered. When on the road for official events, I was terrified of missing my alarm in the morning, so I would ask the hotel for a wake-up call, set my cell phone alarm, try to figure out (usually unsuccessfully) how to set the bedside radio alarm clock, and order room service breakfast or coffee to be delivered for a specific time. I apparently have an internal clock of some sort, too, because I'd end up waking up at least ten minutes before all the other alarms sounded off at their scheduled times. Nevertheless, out of an abundance of caution, I set all these safeguards in place to ensure I could call the General with his wake-up call at the proper time.

On one of our trips to China, while saying goodnight the evening before the General's speech, we confirmed I would call him at six the next morning. We had just traveled from the east coast of the United States to Beijing, and jet lag would be playing havoc with our sleep patterns, so a wakeup call would definitely be needed.

In the dark of night, I was in a very deep sleep when I was jarred awake by the hotel phone ringing beside my bed. My heart dropped when to my groggy "Hello" I heard the General's laughing voice say, *"Ha! Caught you! You overslept, didn't you?"* I was mortified and mumbled apologies while scrambling out of bed, saying I would be ready quickly. I hung up and while grabbing my glasses, glanced at the clock.

And I called him right back.

"Sir, you're not wearing your glasses, are you?" I growled.

Silence.

Then, *"Uh, no."*

"Sir! Put on your glasses. Look at the clock. Now tell me what time it is!"

"Uh, hold on. Um… three."

"Right! Goodbye. I will call you at six and not a minute before. Again, goodbye!"

We had great fun catching each other when one of us made a mistake. We even kept score. I think all of us try to take pride in doing our jobs well. In my little world though, I had the added incentive to stay ahead of General Powell. Keeping score was too much fun. Plus, I had the reassurance that he was a firm believer in his own saying that *"Every organization should tolerate rebels who tell the emperor he has no clothes."* I delighted in being a rebel and telling him when he'd goofed.

For the most part, General Powell was punctual, despite an infamous occasion reported by the press when President Bush locked him out of a cabinet meeting for being late. (He was delayed getting to the White House that day due to an international issue in need of tending, of which the President was aware.)

Anyone who has worked overseas or with foreign visitors is surely aware of how cultural attitudes towards time vary from country to country, and sometimes from person to person.

During our time at the Department of State, standard operating procedure required that whenever high-level dignitaries visited the Department for a meeting with the Secretary of State, a senior protocol officer would greet them upon arrival and provide escort until departure. On extraordinarily busy days, it was not uncommon to have so many visits scheduled that the Chief and Deputy Chief, as well as each of the Assistant Chiefs of Protocol (of which I was one) handled multiple VIP visits throughout the day.

One day I was assigned to greet three dignitaries, each sched-uled to arrive at 1:00 pm. Luckily for me, they each had very different attitudes about punctuality:

Former President George H.W. Bush always arrived early.

The Foreign Minister of Israel always arrived exactly on time.

Former President Bill Clinton always arrived late.

Thankfully, each of these notable gentlemen behaved true to form. President Bush arrived fifteen minutes early, the Foreign Minister of Israel arrived exactly on time, and President Clinton fifteen minutes late.

Thinking of this brings to my mind the children's fairy tale, "Goldilocks and the Three Bears." Goldilocks found the bears' respective bowls of porridge to be too hot, too cold, and just right; their chairs to be too big, too small, and just right; and their beds to be too hard, too soft, and just right. In scientific and academic fields, Wikipedia tells us, the state of being not too much, not too little, but just right is known as being in the "Goldilocks Zone." This was exactly where my General liked to be. As this was not the case for two out of three of these dignitaries, of course you can imagine me sprinting back and forth across the State Department's marble lobby in a dress and high heels between arrivals in order to greet and escort each to his respective meeting on behalf of the Secretary.

When I started my career in the 1980s, everything seemed more formal and glamourous than now. Formal occasions were more often "black tie," not the "cocktail" or "business" attire we see now. Even as a very junior protocol officer, there were many occasions when I had to dress very formally to blend in. Any female readers who work in high profile professions may want to take special note of the next few paragraphs for future reference or for a smile of recognition.

Leslie's Wardrobe Selection Method
Like most jobs early in one's career, my government job's salary was meager. So I had to add long gowns to my work wardrobe as inexpensively as possible.

Often when on duty at one of these special occasions, no matter how dressed up I was, my responsibilities required doing things more suited to sportswear and definitely *not* suited to silk and satin. To maximize my investment, I developed a routine before purchasing anything for work (one which I still follow), and gave the clothing a "stress test" in the changing room. Many dresses, gowns, and pantsuits have been rejected over the years when they failed any of the following criteria:

- *Can I run in it?* I have had to chase motorcades and taxiing airplanes, and I've sprinted the length of stages behind the curtains.

- *Can I jump in it?* I've often had to jump up from a seated position in the back of the room and jump over rain-filled runway potholes in developing countries.

- *Can I bend low in it?* This is a real necessity when picking up accumulations of gifts and whatnot to carry to the car or plane.

- *Can I get in and out of a car quickly and gracefully in it?* Staff cars are often less than comfortable and stretch limousines (or, as the General called them, "awful prom cars") are absolutely the worst of all. And finally,

- *Can the outfit be packed into a suitcase without being unpacked later horribly wrinkled?* With constant travel issues, prep time is often limited.

Like the swan gliding on the surface of a tranquil lake, it's best to appear calm and graceful on the surface even if the mission requires paddling for dear life underneath.

Many years ago, on an international trip to Asia, we had to stop first for an event in York, England, and our baggage didn't make it onto our connecting flight out of London. While our bags were easily traceable and the airline had no problem delivering them to our hotel, they did not arrive in time to prepare for the black-tie event the night of our arrival.

If you are a world-renowned and beloved senior statesman like General Powell, you will be forgiven for showing up at a black-tie event at the castle of a minor nobleman looking like you slept in your suit (which he had) crossing the Atlantic Ocean.

But as the classic aide-de-camp and spear-catching assistant, my looking like something the cat dragged in would not be so readily forgotten or forgiven. Thankfully, with a little sleight of hand I fit in with the castle crowd far better than he did. My silk blouse and black tailored slacks worn without my wrinkled blazer were dressed up sufficiently with the twinkly jewelry stashed away in my carry-on luggage (as one should never *ever* pack jewelry in checked bags). After a few moments in front of a mirror to add a little extra magic, I transformed myself into someone who would blend in with the dinner's elegantly dressed guests, unlike my notably rumpled General.

Like a chameleon fading into its surroundings, I was wallpaper: there to help and enhance the setting or situation, but in the background and mostly ignored. I was happy in the shadows, not distracting from the important and sometimes historic work taking place around the General.

Our awkward beginning may have required some painful love notes, but over the years, we made each other smart by developing tricks of the trade that served us both well.

And we had fun.

3.

Stagecraft

"Trust is the essence of leadership."
—Colin Powell

There is a terrific old Far Side cartoon depicting a herd of sheep at a cocktail party while in the background a dog stands in the doorway about to enter the room. A sheep in the foreground says to his buddy, "Henry! Our party's total chaos! No one knows when to eat, where to stand, what to… Oh, thank goodness! Here comes a border collie!"

Event planners, advance teams, and protocol professionals know the importance of keeping the boss (whether as the honored guest or the host) smart, well informed, moving, and on schedule. We are the elves behind the scenes working the magic, the conductors keeping the trains on time, and sometimes, yes, the border collies herding the sheep.

Over the years, General Powell and I established a way of communicating that would do any professional baseball catcher proud. For VIP cocktail receptions, we'd enter the room, and I would immediately fade into the crowd but within his line of sight. I could pass him a drink and take it from him before anyone noticed. To discourage people from swarming him or trying to grab and spin him (which he *hated*), I would run interference and body block or distract. He was a master of working a room and could successfully greet everyone in the room quicker and more gracefully than it took to wait for someone to introduce him. Though I stayed in the background, I was always positioned to read the expression on his face or his hand gestures and so know the need of the moment. Like the spies in old Cold War movies passing palmed messages, I could easily slip him small notes with scribbled last-minute updates as needed.

If someone caught me doing this, usually it was with incredulity that we could communicate so smoothly and with so little notice. We had it down to a well-rehearsed dance and with a nod of my head I could get him to follow me without anyone else being aware. Even when I was out of his field of view he'd still know where I was, as if he had eyes in the back of his head. When the time came to transition to the next event on the agenda or move somewhere else, he knew it was time as soon as I shifted positions and caught his eye. Whenever my contacts within the organization hosting the event were overwhelmed with the task of moving the guests from one event (e.g., a VIP reception) to another (e.g., the dinner), I would whisper reassurance to them that when they were ready to get the multitude to the next venue I'd simply signal the General to proceed and the crowd would follow.

And it was true. No matter how frustrated my counterpart might become while trying to herd the masses, once the word was given, I could turn the General into the Pied Piper of the room with a simple gesture, and everyone followed dutifully behind. With the host of the event acting as his escort, the General's movement would break the impasse.

Of all the gestures, signals, and signs we had between us, the best of all was the ear tug. Shortly after the General took to any stage, he at some point would very subtly and gently tug at his ear like Carol Burnett in her old television shows, a gesture likely unnoticed by most people watching. Of course, for the big nationally televised events such as the annual National Memorial Day concerts, his children and grandchildren and other loved ones appreciated the gesture as well, but it was a gesture I cherished each time he appeared on the speaking circuit: Once he took center stage or stood behind the lectern, as soon as he and I made eye contact in even the most crowded room, he would touch his ear, confirming he had spotted me; I would respond in kind, and we would both know it was now "show time!"

Watch old recordings of speeches and concerts, look for the ear tug and know it still makes me smile and always will.

* * *

On the speaking circuit before the start of the coronavirus pandemic, an event usually included a photo opportunity with the General for VIP guests. If I had a dime for every photo-op I've staged over the years, I would surely have collected enough to take a very nice (and very long) vacation in some lovely corner of the world.

For the most part, General Powell did not mind photo-ops, provided they were done his way. (As I always said, "Once a General, always a General.") His rules usually made perfect sense. Many a group after an event would admit that, once they'd mastered his "four-star" rules, they planned to use them from then on, as these rules made things flow much more smoothly. Whenever

I met professional photographers who had photographed the General before, they, too, would reassure me that the General's rules were the best:

> *From the left*: Guests were to be always, always, *always* lined up beside him just outside of the camera shot, receiving-line style, coming to him from his left and exiting to his right. Imagine you are General Powell and in receiving each guest, you naturally extend your right hand to shake the hand of the guest and then you and the guest (while shaking hands) face the camera and smile. Once the picture is taken, you can gently pull the guest to exit from your right and you are ready for the next guest. My rule of thumb was to allow 30 minutes for 100 pictures (which with couples meant 200 individuals). Sometimes, if I had a particularly good photographer and several assistants to manage the line, the General and I could successfully run over 300 individuals through a photo-op in a half hour.

> *Individual photos not group shots*: Don't ever let anyone tell you taking group shots is faster. It is always easier and quicker to do individual photos than small groups. No matter how sophisticated a group is, getting small groups of people into place is like shoveling fog.

> *Just shoot*: Never ever let the photographer count to three. What an easy way to waste time.

Over the years and the thousands of speeches the General gave, stagecraft became a second language to us both and we became experts on elaborate productions involving platforms and risers, image magnification screens, speakers, piping and drape, house lights, microphones, spotlights, and all the other equipment and accoutrement that go into the creation of an event. We could differentiate between organizations that used skilled teams to handle the logistics and those that just "winged it." When the event teams seemed to need assistance (or said assistance was welcomed), the General told his hosts, "Just let Leslie show them how," and off I would go, in command.

Regardless, the smartest bear in the woods (i.e., General Powell) knew from experience what worked best in all aspects of stagecraft— and I always try to pass along this knowledge to anyone who will listen or read:

Lavalier microphones: Keep in mind a lavalier microphone is most effective when positioned as close to the speaker's mouth as possible. At a Latin American business conference for an international bank, General Powell was seated on stage for a fireside-chat style discussion with the host of the event, the leader of the bank. The General's lavalier microphone was perfectly positioned towards the top of his tie and therefore, right under and close to his mouth. Unfortunately, the international banker positioned his on his lapel, but on the opposite side from which he would turn his head when asking a question. As a result, although the audience could easily hear the General's side of the discussion, they couldn't hear the banker posing the questions. The poor banker came across as an overwhelmed novice. The General, by contrast, appeared clearly in charge and the one the audience could choose to follow.

Image magnification (IMAG) screens: Big rooms that accommodate large crowds can benefit from IMAG screens, but proportions can make a big difference. Too often screens are not large enough to be as effective as they should be. It's frustrating when people in the back of a room can't see. General Powell liked to use IMAG screens to his advantage by maximizing his facial expressions, knowing a look was worth a thousand words.

Interpretation equipment: Always, always, *always* make sure headsets being used for interpretation are functional well in advance. Having a principal on stage struggling with a broken piece of equipment is embarrassing for everyone. Also, make sure instructions on how to use the equipment are clear.

Stage speakers: Microphones are often passed through an audience for asking questions of those on stage. It's easy to forget that the speakers meant to project what is said by the principals are facing the audience and will not necessarily project back to those on stage. To counter this, a small speaker known as a "confidence speaker" should be placed on the stage facing the stage participants. General Powell had hearing loss (what I'd termed "infantry ears") from his many years in the military and so he benefited from the additional speaker.

Seating: General Powell often appeared on the international speaker circuit with another former U.S. Secretary of State, his good friend, Dr. Madeleine K. Albright. They were fabulous together—brilliant, witty, charming, and inspiring in representing their sometimes opposite and sometimes shared viewpoints. Seating them on stage was a challenge though, as the General was over six feet tall and Dr. Albright barely five feet. With almost a foot difference in their heights, staging arrangements always included having a decorative pillow added to the back of her chair so she was not at a disadvantage or uncomfortable in her seat.

Many readers will remember the infamous "talking hat" incident that took place during the Welcome Ceremony on the South Lawn of the White House during a State Visit in 1991. On this occasion, it was observed around the world that although the podium's lectern had been perfectly positioned for the very tall then President of the United States, George H. W. Bush, it was not at all positioned well for Her Majesty Queen Elizabeth II. As soon as the Queen came to the lectern, all that could be seen above the lectern's attached microphone was her hat. Although there was a small step built into the lectern base, it had not been extended for her.

Introductions: Introductions should be short and to the point. I cannot think of a single time a long introduction was ever necessary or appreciated. If long biographical information is needed to be imparted to an audience, it likely should be provided by other means—perhaps written in a program (if written programs are provided) or given in some other form in advance. For someone of General Powell's storied and exemplary resume, an audience could be put to sleep while listening to someone recite the history lesson of the General's long list of accomplishments. Long introductions usually end up being more about the introducer than they are about the person being introduced.

Entrances and Exits: It may sound obvious, but make sure getting on and off stage is easy. There may be harsh stage lights shining in the faces of the leaders on stage, making it hard to see without stumbling. Transitioning from a brightly lit stage to a darkened backstage area may be equally disorienting. Also, if one must go up or down stairs attached to a stage, there should be a handrail present, but if not, have someone there to offer an arm for support, thus alleviating any possible danger of stumbling.

Lecterns: Despite the fact that production companies sometimes like the artistic appeal of modern lecterns (e.g., clear, minimalistic, or futuristic), these stylistic marvels are often not "user friendly." If a speaker needs to use notes, then the top of the lectern needs to have a lip so the notes don't fall to the floor. There also needs to be a light to illumine those notes—and the positioning of any attached microphone should not cast a shadow that makes the notes unreadable. I prefer a solid lectern, as no one in an audience needs to be distracted by how a speaker stands. As I have said before, General Powell rarely used notes, but sometimes official staging required him to stand behind a lectern that had been put in place for other speakers at the event.

Spotlights: General Powell was a master communicator from any stage but especially when he could see his audience. I would work with the AV folk to make sure the house lights were up as much as possible (at least up as high as they could be without interfering with the IMAGs). He wanted to make direct eye contact with the audience, as that direct connection helped him work his magic. Equally important though was to make sure the spotlights on stage weren't angled directly into his eyes like, as he would say, "painful klieg lights from an oncoming train."

Appearances matter: Appearances can significantly affect how an event's success is judged. Whether it's viewed in person or afterward in photographs, the physical appearance of a government or organization leader, or even a staffer in the background, can have a dramatic effect on how the occasion is perceived.

Consider an image that will always be a part of the history books, depicting the historic meeting in October 1986 of then President of the United States Ronald Reagan and the Secretary General of the Soviet Union Mikhail Gorbachev at the Reykjavik Summit. Although the expectations for the political success of the summit were low, every aspect of this meeting of the leaders of the world's superpowers at the height of the Cold War had a significant impact on public perception. When the two men greeted each other on the steps of Hofdi House, the world saw two very different people: The Soviet Secretary General wearing a coat and looking decidedly cold and the American President dressed in nothing more than his business suit, looking quite comfortable.

The historians will debate and interpret over time all the decisions and compromises and policies that led to an end to the Cold War. However, for that one moment in time, the hale and hearty image of the American leader standing with the shivering Russian leader bundled up in a coat beside him certainly made an impression on how the leaders were seen in the media on that occasion.

Similarly, many years later, I remember worrying over seeing a picture in the news of then Vice President of the United States Dick Cheney at an international summit, dressed in a hooded parka and snow boots while all other leaders in the group were dressed in street shoes, suits, and dress coats.

In 1998, because he had held the most senior position in the U.S. military, General Powell was asked to introduce two of the Best Picture nominees at the Academy Awards: *Saving Private Ryan* and *The Thin Red Line*, as each depicted significant military stories from World War II. As unusual as it was for Hollywood to embrace and showcase one of our most notable military veterans, General Powell accepted the call to introduce both movies at the televised award ceremonies and did a marvelous job. What the viewing public did not know was during the rehearsals, the show producers told General Powell that when watching him walk onto the stage they realized he had that *je ne sais quoi* that allowed him to command the room simply with his presence. They explained the way he carried himself was something many celebrities, actors, and presenters paid a lot of money to learn how to do. And he had a weight of presence that could not be bought, bottled, or sold. The producers were in awe.

We often keep an eye on how our leaders present themselves. With camera phones so ubiquitous these days, it's best not to look disheveled while walking off a plane or scrambling for loose papers beside an official. Yes, I always viewed my role with General Powell as being in the background. Even so, in representing him I was ever mindful of appropriate manner and dress.

* * *

During a Q&A session following a National Symphony Orchestra Pops Concert, a friend of General Powell's, the late American composer and conductor Marvin Hamlisch, explained the reason he had named his award-winning musical *A Chorus Line* rather than *Chorus Line* (which had been his first plan). He knew that including "A" in the title would ensure his show always appeared at the top of theater listings. With a twinkle in his eye, he admitted that doing so was a trick that would allow his show to always appear before many other fabulous shows—e.g., *Aida, Aladdin, American in Paris, Annie,* and *Annie Get Your Gun,* etc. To theater fans, *A Chorus Line,* seems the perfect title because it describes the musical and film. To the composer, it was a perfect title because it allowed him to manipulate its listing to pay dividends ever after.

General Powell and I were likewise masters at manipulation. I could always pull my event contact into my confidence and share some trick to the staging or event flow that would make the hosting organization look fabulous while keeping the General happy. As the saying goes, we could "maximize a win-win situation" for all involved.

For every event that requires intricate seating of dignitaries and guests, a bit of art and science to choreograph the seating is also required, balancing the rules of precedence while allowing for social and civil niceties. The task can furrow the brow of the most seasoned host.

One of the most frustrating challenges any host or hostess may face is having a guest for a seated meal arrive late or, worse, be a "no show." When told this has happened, I've been known to utter in my best southern drawl, "Well, obviously his momma didn't raise him right." Of course, I mean it in jest and only say it amongst my equally frustrated colleagues to provide a bit of comic relief as we all then scramble to rearrange the seating to reflect the errant guest's absence.

While a "no show" for an official meal is problematic, it's particularly disruptive when that guest was to be seated at the head table. During his years as Secretary of State, General Powell and I routinely had to deal with the fact that government leaders from the legislative branch were and are notorious for canceling at the last minute or simply not showing up (or even, worst of all, sending a staff member in their place). Unfortunately, due to their titles and ranks in the official U.S. Order of Precedence list, their seating placement at the head table or a comparable table of rank often was required. Consequently, their absences left glaringly obvious and embarrassingly empty seats.

Yes, having wait staff simply pull an empty place setting while rearranging the rest of the table was sometimes an option. However, sometimes circumstances required other ways of dealing with the challenge.

One of our best solutions was to designate a couple of people who could be on standby to "fill in." As most of our entertaining was done in the State Department's 8th floor Diplomatic Reception Rooms, so beautifully appointed and decorated with 18th century American antiques, we could often tap the State Department's curator, Gail Serfaty, and her pool of official donors to step into this role. Similarly, we could tap other members of an unofficial "friends and family" list that might include other senior Department of State officials (those not already seated prominently) and even senior protocol officers—any of whom could rise to the occasion, look the part, and socially engage appropriately.

Any one of us can be called away for an emergency or have a legitimate conflict precluding us (or our principals) from attending a previously accepted event, but when that happens, it is an absolute necessity to alert those hosting the event as soon as possible. Think of it as a gift to those in charge so they have time to rearrange their carefully planned tables or to draft their "filler-inners" to slip into the empty seats with grace.

Secretary Powell was always the epitome of the perfect host. Unfortunately, not every guest remembers to be the perfect guest.

* * *

Having a trick up his sleeve to take an audience—and most especially his hosts—by surprise was something General Powell relished. Yes, he always delivered an excellent speech, providing great substantive words of wisdom, but he liked to punctuate his presentation with something unexpected. Once, when delivering the keynote speech to a national drugstore association, in his opening remarks he slowly and dramatically pulled from his pocket a receipt several feet long which he had recently received checking out at his local drugstore. At an event in Mexico for Carlos Slim, at the time the wealthiest person in the world, both General Powell and Mario Andretti, one of the most successful drivers ever in motorsports, were scheduled to deliver keynote speeches. At the last minute, General Powell had me scramble to get the AV team to project pictures of him driving the Indy 500 pace car, all in hopes of leaving Mario Andretti speechless. In so doing, he also left the racecar aficionados in the audience holding their sides with laughter.

I once participated in a speaker series held by the Tuckahoe Women's Club in Richmond, Virginia. Naturally, they had really wanted General Powell to speak but he was not available, so they settled on me. Clearly, it was a case of apples and oranges, but I accepted the invitation nonetheless. As I was born in Richmond and as relatives on both sides of my family still lived there, this was a special event for me. Several cousins, aunts, an uncle, and additional extended family members joined my mother for the occasion, all having never heard me speak before. An unexpected additional treat was the fact that a whole bus load of my mother's friends from her high school graduating class came from a nearby senior living community specifically for the chance to hear "Margaret's daughter" give a speech called "The Gift of Protocol," that would focus on my many years with General Powell.

The several hundred audience members—my extended family included—all may have had knowledge of what protocol is in a very general sense (this being a ladies' club in Virginia, most were well-versed in etiquette), but they likely did not come for the program understanding the significance of protocol in all aspects of life, not just on the international stage. Knowing this, I planned my presentation to be as entertaining as I could so that guests would leave inspired and encouraged.

Having by that time been at the General's side for over two decades of his speaking career, I had absorbed his penchant for using some trick to engage the audience from the earliest moments on stage. I discovered that during the coffee hour prior to the start of the program there was a live pianist on stage playing show tunes and songs from *The Great American Songbook*. Once I learned this, I discarded what I had planned as my opening comments. Instead, while the guests were still enjoying coffee and conversation, I tiptoed onto the stage and softly asked the pianist if she knew a particular song, and if so, could she—would she—please play a few bars immediately following my introduction. She was hesitant until I shared with her (with the help of a quick Google and YouTube search) a snippet of Frank Sinatra singing the song I wanted. Though still a bit puzzled, she agreed to play my requested "walk-on" music.

Sure enough, as soon as the chairwoman of the event finished delivering my official introduction, from the grand piano could be heard the opening notes of the Rodgers and Hart song, "The Lady is a Tramp."

As you can imagine once the polite applause that follows any introduction died down, I heard chuckles and even some gasps as those in the audience slowly recognized the song and its lyrics. (And I am sure you can imagine the stunned look on the faces of my relatives—most especially my mother—sitting in the front rows.)

And with that, I sashayed to the front of the stage with a big smile. I reassured them the song choice was intentional as it represented a perfect example of the importance of stagecraft and how every detail matters, then I segued into a story:

Many may remember the unfortunate faux pas that happened during the State Visit of Her Majesty Queen Elizabeth II following the dinner given in her honor by the President of the United States and First Lady Betty Ford. As with many State Dinners, the after-dinner entertainment at the White House included dancing to music provided by "The President's Own," the United States Marine Band and Marine Chamber Orchestra, an ensemble of truly extraordinary musicians with a vast command and repertoire of music. It's therefore easy to imagine how people cringed when "The Lady is a Tramp" was played while Her Majesty was on the dance floor in the arms of President Ford!

For the rest of my speech, I spoke about protocol mishaps and traveling the world with General Powell, sharing tales that made the audience laugh and others that made them cry.

As soon as I finished the event, I called the General to report how it went, as he had been a part of my planning since I'd accepted the invitation. After I told him of my last-minute inspiration to add "The Lady is a Tramp" piece to my intro, he responded, "Atta Girl! Chip off the ol' block!"

Indeed, no higher praise was possible.

4.

Master Communicator

*"The freedom to be your best means nothing unless
you are willing to do your best."*
—Colin Powell

The only time I was ever afraid while traveling with General Powell was in a car leaving an airport in Nigeria. We were traveling across town from an international airport to a regional one to catch a flight to a smaller city. We made slow progress, as the roads were packed with people, including several men in fatigues carrying what looked to me like machine guns, walking alongside and occasionally touching our car. I have no idea if this heavy traffic was typical for this time of the day or week, or if there had been some event causing the congestion, but I was blissfully unconcerned—until General Powell casually pulled my purse from my lap and slowly placed it under his feet. He did not say a word, catch my eye, or even change his facial expression—but his message was chilling and clear. His simple protective gesture clarified the danger we were in.

By word or gesture, he was always a master communicator.

* * *

At the end of my ballet classes growing up, my teachers closed each class with a specially choreographed floor exercise known as "the ritual of the reverence," which in essence was a wordless thank you expressed through carefully choreographed dance steps to accompanying music.

I cannot imagine the General in a ballet class, but the ritual of the reverence well describes his insistence on always expressing his gratitude to those around him. As with most celebrities, our entrances into venues often required going through loading docks, back hallways, and kitchens. He was always eager to say hello and thank you to the chefs, wait staff, and backstage workers toiling hard behind the scenes. Likewise, he was always ready to acknowledge those whose careful attention eased his way through airports and private hangars. He was as quick to write a thank-you note to those in support roles as to his hosts. And in response to the hundreds if not thousands of invitations he constantly received, his note of regret always included an expression of gratitude for being invited.

* * *

Many years ago, as part of a two-year international tour to raise money for the People's Princess Charitable Foundation, Inc., twenty gowns worn by Diana, Princess of Wales, were on display for several weeks at the Ronald Reagan Building in Washington, D.C. Tickets allowed members of the public to enter a darkened hall and view these beautiful dresses displayed in spotlighted glass cases. I no longer remember how or why I was a docent for one of the days of the tour, but I was given some basic information to memorize about the gowns so, if asked, I could answer intelligently.

My final group for the day was a group of eight 20-something-year-old young men who bounded through the entrance and asked if I would give them a personal tour. I said I'd be happy to answer their questions, but the exhibit was self-guided, and they could view at their leisure. They persisted however, crowding around me, and asked again. I demurred, saying my knowledge could not be as enthralling as whatever they imagined. The self-appointed spokesman of the group teasingly responded, "Just flaunt your knowledge, baby!"

We all laughed, then the group leader said no matter how limited I thought my knowledge, it was exponentially more than whatever they knew about royal gowns, and they were eager to learn anything I was willing to share. I surrendered to their charm, and with an added skip to my step and a twinkle in my eye, in the manner of Scheherazade I gave these beguiling rogues an animated tour, weaving the limited facts I had into colorful vignettes describing the occasions at which the gowns were worn.

Often before large speaking events, there would be smaller VIP lunches or dinners giving the organization's top donors, sponsors, and leadership an opportunity to have exclusive time with General Powell. Even though everyone attending the meal function would have the opportunity for a picture with him, only a few were seated at his table. Those not so fortunate were usually disappointed in not having the added luster of being entertained by him while breaking bread together.

As his assistant, I never assumed I would be seated at the event although often our hosts would graciously seat me anyway. In those cases, I always reassured them there was no need for me to be placed with the General at the head table, saying they should give the "good seat" to someone important in the group instead. As long as I could be seen by General Powell, I could be seated elsewhere.

When seated away from the dignitaries, I would entertain my tablemates with inside stories to lessen their disappointment of not sharing a table with the General. With a few well-chosen anecdotes my companions would soon be laughing, enthralled with my tales of life on the road with *the* General Powell. To help the role I was playing, the General would play along and tell my tablemates in a mock scolding tone, "Don't believe a word she says—it's not true!" Or he would call out, "I want to be at the fun table!" letting them know they would still be entertained, even if not by him, and that my table might in the end be more fun. Whichever way, he was communicating a gift of a little extra attention to those seated with me *and* letting his hosts know he appreciated the guests at all the tables, not just the VIPs. He had complete confidence I would paint stories revealing only what he wanted or did not mind being shared, and we would play up my ability to just "flaunt my knowledge" of him and entertain the guests at "the fun table."

Perception is everything and he taught me well.

* * *

General Powell may not have been fluent in multiple languages, but he was quick to master the appropriate words for thank you in the language of his visitor or the country he was visiting. After many trips with him to South Korea, even I learned to share a sincere "*gamsahapnida*" to convey my gratitude to those helping us, and I still practice whenever I visit my local dry cleaner, which is owned by a charming couple from Seoul.

Although I took German in junior and senior high school, it was a couple decades before I met any native speakers, and by then I had lost whatever minimal proficiency I'd once had to "*sprechen Deutsch*." Similarly, I'd taken an immersion crash course in French in preparation for a rewarding five years working for a U.S.-based foundation affiliated with a museum in Normandy, France—and yet I've only ever mastered what I call consumer French. That is to say, although I can speak with hotel and restaurant staff, police officers, shopkeepers, and the like, I would be hard pressed to have an intelligent conversation about the meaning of life with a native speaker. Fortunately, during the many months I lived in France, I was usually surrounded by people who were bilingual and preferred to speak English rather than suffer my attempts to *parler français*.

I am in awe of anyone who is multilingual and figuratively tip my hat to anyone who speaks more than one language fluently, as that person is far more accomplished than I. Likewise, I will forever be in awe of professional translators and interpreters, especially those who assisted the General through the years.

In June 2018, National Public Radio (NPR) released a report called "The Pressures of Being an Interpreter at a High-Stakes Summit." Online was a link to the text of the broadcast, which included photographs of two interpreters with whom General Powell and I had worked over the years, specifically head of interpretation services at the U.S. Department of State, Stephanie van Reigersberg, and Soviet Pavel Palazhchenko. In the report, journalist Danny Hajek revealed some interesting examples of occasions where mistakes in interpretation could have had dire repercussions. Hajek correctly states that in high-level meetings, "interpreters face the pressures of global diplomacy. Every word matters, and a slip-up can have monumental consequences."

Very true.

And yet one account of an interpretation mishap stayed with me long after I read about it, thanks to the wisdom of the leaders involved. The story describes a nuclear negotiation between U.S. President George H.W. Bush and Soviet leader Mikhail Gorbachev during the Cold War. The Soviet interpreter, Igor Korchilov, incorrectly used the word "verifying" instead of "verified," a significant error when used in conversations about the arms control treaty being discussed. Despite the ramifications his mistake could have had on the negotiations (if not history itself), his apologies to both leaders caused each to respond with diplomatic restraint and human understanding. President Bush reassured him with a bit of understatement, saying, "[T]he good news is that you didn't start World War III." Meanwhile, Soviet leader Gorbachev put everything into perspective, saying, "[D]on't worry, Igor. Only those who do nothing make no mistakes."

What a comfort those words are: *Only those who do nothing make no mistakes.*

No matter where we traveled, General Powell was appreciative of those who worked tirelessly to ensure accuracy in spoken and written word.

Every now and then, something would come up in popular culture that would be as discordant to the General as fingernails on a chalkboard. Whenever that happened, he was quick to give a lecture (er, lesson) to correct the mistake.

One case in point: "*over and out.*"

The General was always quick to quote from movies and would often reference "Cool Hand Luke," quoting the classic line, "What we've got here is a failure to communicate." However, whenever he would hear someone say "over and out," he would lecture whomever happened to be in earshot, saying that anyone who has heard actors dramatically say that phrase on the radio has heard a completely illogical phrase. To say "over" means you are turning the communication over to the other person for a response. To say "and out" means you are closing the communication and turning off the radio. This would mean that the poor person to whom you have turned "over" the communication is now talking on a severed communication line, because you have just dropped the radio link.

In response to this tutorial on radio protocol, I reassured General Powell that I'd learned the proper techniques during my early adventures as a Visits Officer, when he was the National Security Advisor. In those days, we had been issued portable phones and two-way radios (i.e., walkie-talkies) as big and heavy as bricks, and were taught to use proper radio terminology. When initiating contact, we'd state the name of the person we were trying to reach twice, then say our name once: "Julie, Julie. Leslie." No need for additional words—no "please," no "come in," no "Who's on the line?" Just, "Julie, Julie. Leslie," to which Julie would reply, "Go for Julie," or "Julie, over." Walkie-talkie dialogue is most effective when it conveys succinct information and gives brief, clear commands. As the lingo is different from normal speech, the speakers need to understand the rules to function.

When I explained this to the General, I was delighted to hear I'd passed his test.

We constantly flinched at the poor communication styles of some clients and contacts. Think of acronyms and online slang. Whatever the industry, acronyms are not necessarily known or understood by those outside that culture. Furthermore, "IDK" and "LOL" may be commonly used to respectively express "I don't know" and "laugh out loud" when communicating on social media, but neither is appropriate in official exchanges.

Likewise, think of idioms. When working with foreign delegations, it is important to avoid colloquial language that may not translate well. Several years ago at an annual education forum for Protocol & Diplomacy International–Protocol Officers Association (PDI-POA), a colleague from China laughingly explained he was shocked when told he could get a "head shot" at the conference. It took a bit of explaining before he understood this meant he could get a portrait taken by a professional photographer, not that he could be shot in the head.

Over the years, the General and I developed our own shorthand: a way of communicating in code which we would understand and others would not unless we provided a tutorial. We never assumed an abbreviation or acronym was understood by someone else unless we had used the code with them before.

From the moment most of us learn to talk, we learn an appropriate response in English to "Thank you" is simply "You're welcome." I am not sure when or why it became common practice, but often these days instead of hearing "You're welcome," I hear "Not a problem" or "No problem" or even worse, "No probs." It may not have bothered General Powell as much as it did me, but he would patiently listen to me squawk about someone saying "Not a problem" in response to my "Thank you," as if my expression of gratitude was being taken as an apology for causing a problem and I needed assurance from the person that it was not.

Ever the diplomat, General Powell always adapted his word choice, tone, and cadence to his audience. Whether speaking one-on-one with a counterpart through an interpreter, or from a stage to a vast ballroom filled with attentive conference attendees, he was the master of his message.

Sitting beside General Powell in an audience was also a lesson in communication and a reminder that the demeanor of an audience member can make a difference to those on stage. He was always an attentive listener and would absorb what he heard from previous speakers so he could use it in his remarks when it was his turn to take the stage, wowing the audience with his added knowledge.

Traveling around the world on the international speaking circuit for decades with General Powell, I had the good fortune of hearing many terrific speakers give stirring speeches that motivated and inspired audiences. Whether chiefs of state, community leaders, college presidents, or celebrities from the arts and entertainment world, many a gifted speaker has moved the General and me to tears or laughter or action (and sometimes all three) with their skilled oratory and passion.

Unfortunately, I can say the same about the less gifted speakers we had the misfortune of hearing. Having a speaker move an audience to tears, laughter, or action from a poor performance on stage is painfully embarrassing.

I remember one occasion when a particular leader—an expert in his field—gave a presentation that was just plain awful. Whether he was ill prepared, having a bad day, or his message was no longer relevant, his delivery left the audience disgruntled and unhappy.

Because of my role at this event, I was seated in the front row and knew my reactions and facial expressions were clearly visible to the speaker. Knowing this, I did everything I could to mask my true reaction to his dismal talk. Consequently, I felt like a complete phony at the end of the program when he personally thanked me, saying how grateful he was for my encouraging smile during his speech because it gave him a confidence he wished he could find in every audience. If he found encouragement in my faked enthusiasm, I'd hate to think how bad his speech would have been without it.

Everything about the experience reminded me how skilled General Powell was, always as prepared and "smart" as he could be for every event. Part of the reason for this speaker's failure had been that he did not know his audience. It was also a good reminder of what the General knew: we are never just a face in the crowd. Body language and facial expressions can support a speaker who just might need it at that moment.

* * *

Once he left the U.S. State Department and returned to private life, General Powell did not utilize a detail or security team. He always explained that there is no easier way to call attention to oneself than to be surrounded by an armed entourage. How much easier it is to be safe moving around unnoticed without it.

Even so, there were tricks those of us closest to him developed after his retirement that made movement easier. It was a constant challenge to travel anywhere in public. When trying to stick to a tightly planned schedule, wading through a crowded lobby or airport invariably slowed us down, as people always wanted to stop him for an autograph, a photograph (or one of those dreaded selfies), a handshake, or a stolen hug.

He may have been a master communicator, but these situations required more than his smooth talking. To keep him safe and on time, he and I developed a repertoire of techniques to keep us on schedule:

Keep moving: One of the best ways to maneuver through a crowd we could not avoid was to simply keep moving and not make eye contact. Most people are so caught up in their own worlds they do not notice who is around them. If we did not settle in one place, General Powell often could slip through before being spotted.

Look fierce: When he was recognized, I could usually stop over-enthusiastic celebrity seekers, barreling towards us with camera phones clutched in their hands, just by shaking my head and frowning. Few dared go further.

Know your choreography: When escorting the General in public places, I would whisper something as simple as, "Your ten o'clock," to alert him someone was headed towards us from the left up ahead. I would then casually cross in front of him so that the approaching individual would have to get through me to get to him. I am only average height so I was not likely to scare away people who were truly on a mission to engage the General, but I could usually deflect most from pursuing their goals.

Avoid the avalanche: The biggest challenge was trying to prevent a situation from growing from a snowball into an avalanche. This was often when someone wanted something signed— once others in the crowd saw the General sign one person's item, crowds quickly formed wanting the same. To avoid this, when someone would make the initial request, I would ask that person to give me the item so the General could sign it out of the public eye and then I'd return it to the requestor afterwards. That way, we were able to please the one person without attracting a mob.

* * *

On several occasions, General Powell called out to me from across the room at a cocktail party, saying, "Leslie, what's that weird superpower you have? Here, tell them." To which I'd respond, "What color is the letter E? How about the color of the number three?"

I know most people reading those two sentences have no idea how to answer. For me though, the letter E is a dark fuchsia, almost a red color, and the number three is a bright green (think of the color of Kermit the Frog). I can go down the whole alphabet and count to ten telling you the color of each letter and number. I can also tell you that the days of the week read from right to left when I try to visualize them, and the months of the year form a double helix with January at the top, August at the bottom, with April and October crossing in the middle.

I have something shared by only 3 to 5 percent of the population, called synesthesia, a neurological condition in which stimulation of one sensory or cognitive pathway also stimulates another. Where I see letters and numbers in color, other synesthetes taste or hear colors or experience many other interesting and perplexing combinations of sensory perceptions.

Although I doubt my synesthesia provides me superpowers, many a time the General treated it as if it did and it provided a humorous if not interesting way to communicate.

And then there was my raised eyebrow. When I wanted the General to behave, I would simply raise one eyebrow and look at him over my glasses. Like an errant schoolboy cringing away from an old-fashioned schoolmarm's admonishing stare, he would inevitably laugh and exclaim, "Wait! What did I do this time? Don't give me that look! What have I done?"

Whether it was a look and gesture from the General, or a raised eyebrow from me, the joy of communication was always far more than words.

5.

Home Away From Home

"I am always happy to be out where I can observe all the myriad varieties of Americans. And I love being on the speaking circuit, or in schools, Boys and Girls Clubs, charity events, and all the other wonderful activities going on around our nation."
—Colin Powell, "It Worked for Me," p. 256

While traveling so much for speaking engagements there were usually big blocks of time spent in hotels between events or before catching the next plane or train. General Powell was a voracious reader—at home, he read five newspapers every day, navigated around the internet for headlines, and kept current on recent bestsellers. Even on the road, he was certain to stay as current as possible on his reading, surfing or watching whatever was at hand. In addition, he would call his best friends—his consiglieres, his lieutenants—for the inside scoop, multiple times a day.

He channel surfed all the news shows, but once he'd absorbed what was relevant, he would dismiss the talking heads, knowing such shows were driven more by market share and advertising dollars than straight news. He was keenly interested in watching the foreign news channels, for even though they had their own agendas, they were at least less driven by the personalities and entertainers who too often masquerade as journalists on cable channels in the United States.

His thirst for staying up to date was insatiable.

Even so, once he'd absorbed all he could for the day, General Powell would turn to a diverse array of shows for background noise while he worked on his computer or phone. I watched my first televised boxing match while on the road with him. (I didn't like it.) Likewise, I watched the only episodes I have ever watched of *Pawn Stars* and the World Wide Wrestling Federation. (I didn't like those either.) Despite my disinterest in these programs, the General tried to educate me on the finer points of each, claiming they provided interesting studies in human behavior. Although I have a degree in psychology, I would not use any of these shows for behavioral analysis, they being too yawn inducing for me. I much preferred the National Geographic and Animal Planet shows he liked. And the movies! He loved old movies and musicals.

Before each event that required us to overnight at a hotel, I would share with my event contacts the secret code name they should give the hotel as an alias for his room reservation. By using a pseudonym, the hotel front desk personnel could answer truthfully, "There is no one by that name registered with us," when strange people called the hotel asking for Colin Powell. We changed the name we used every couple of years or so and had great fun being creative. The first name I chose was Donald Lockwood, Gene Kelly's character in *Singing in the Rain*. That lasted all of two days until the General decided he felt more like a Richard than a Donald, and so we switched out the first name. Next came Edward Felson. General Powell loved the movie *The Hustler* with Paul Newman and Jackie Gleason. "Fast Eddie" Felson was the character played by Paul Newman and the General could and would quote him with gusto. As much as it might be hard to believe, he also loved the movie *Dirty Dancing*, the dialogue of which we could both quote at length in recitation battles. For that reason, his last secret hotel name was John Houseman—John as a nod to Patrick Swayze's character Johnny, and Houseman as a nod to Jennifer Gray's character, Baby Houseman. For my room down the hall or around the corner, I could of course be registered simply under my name. No need for me to be incognito; I was blissfully unknown.

General Powell preferred avoiding unnecessary pomp and circumstance, and I often had a hard time convincing our hosts that having a delegation greet him at an airport or hotel was not necessary. The General knew our hosts had more important demands on their time than to stand on ceremony someplace waiting for him to arrive. We were relieved and grateful if the front desk simply handed us our room keys.

This was the case late one night in New Orleans. Although the General had given a dinner speech in Tennessee earlier that evening, he was scheduled to attend a breakfast and be the general session keynote speaker at a meeting in Louisiana the next morning, which meant we had to fly by charter plane in the middle of the night. As we expected to arrive at the hotel close to 1:00 am, I insisted that our hosts *not* be there to greet us but that they please just leave everything with the reception desk staff.

When we arrived at the hotel, I parked the General temporarily behind a potted tree (yes, really), grabbed the keys from the front desk, and without further delay steered him to our rooms for the night. Our rooms were adjacent and as we bid our goodnights in the hall, the General entered his room while I fumbled with my card key. Just as I was opening my door, General Powell backed out of his room with a curious look on his face and slowly closed his door while whispering, "There is a naked man in my bed."

My response? "Is he dead?"

General Powell replied he didn't think so, as he thought he saw movement. He then laughed at the absurdity of a dead body being my first thought.

Having established that we did not have a corpse on our hands but rather a living being sans clothing, I pushed General Powell into my room and ordered him not to move while I high-tailed it down to the lobby to get another room.

It's always a good idea to couch startling news with gentle reassurance, so when I reached the front desk I prefaced the report of our predicament with a "Truly, everything is fine, but I need a new room." Despite my carefully phrased introduction, when I shared the reason why, both hotel officials at the desk were on their feet, stumbling over their words to apologize and figure out how this could possibly have happened. I reassured them again that all was indeed fine (and it really did not matter why it had happened), there was no need to find a new room for the General, as he was fine taking mine, just please find another one for me.

Fortunately, once I was given a new room the rest of the night passed uneventfully. The next morning though, when I picked up the General for the scheduled breakfast with our hosts I made him tiptoe out of the room in hopes of not running into the poor previously unclothed soul. Let the poor guy think he had just dreamed of General Powell in his room if there had been any awareness at all on his part.

Many people know from experience the joys and challenges of work-related travel. I suspect fellow globetrotters have developed their own checklist of things to do, pack, and plan for each trip. Others who may not travel themselves may receive and support well-traveled visitors and I'm sure these devoted hosts have their own tried and true checklists for receiving them.

As much as I hope the lists I make—both on the traveling side of things as well as on the receiving end—are thorough and thoughtful, I can still stumble over a detail I missed. Therefore, I am always sympathetic when I'm on the road and discover that others have also.

Many years ago, General Powell and I arrived in Dallas, Texas late one evening after having been on the road for several days of back-to-back events. We were both exhausted and looking forward to a good night's sleep in the hotel arranged for us. It was a lovely four- or five-star hotel where every amenity expected in a luxury hotel was available and the exceptional hotel staff tended to our every need.

After ensuring the General was settled in and bidding good-night to my contact and the hotel staff member who'd escorted me there, alone in my room I prepared for bed. Before I could go to sleep, though, I needed to turn off the bedside stereo the hotel staff had left playing. This being Texas, it was tuned to a festive salsa channel.

Imagine my frustration when I could not figure out how to turn it off, then double that trying to imagine what I felt when I realized I could not even turn the volume down low enough to be nearly muted. The best I could do was to switch the channel to "environmental sounds." Quickly dismissing sounds of thunderstorms and rain forests, I settled on "ocean waves."

What could otherwise be assumed to provide the perfect background soundtrack to lull my exhausted travel-weary self to a quick sleep turned out to be nothing of the sort. Every two minutes or so the sound of the rolling ocean waves was punctuated by the sound of seagulls cawing, followed by a buoy bell ringing, ending with a foghorn blowing, before it all started again with the sound of waves crashing.

All. Night. Long.

Unplugging the infernal machine was not an option as the bedside table and the massive bed were against the wall, blocking the electrical outlets. I also could not find instructions explaining the workings of the fancy sound system. Perhaps I should have called the front desk, but it was the middle of the night, and I did not want to be a bother.

When I met up with the General in the morning, we compared stories. He, too, had been welcomed by festive salsa music and couldn't figure out how to turn it off. For once though, he benefited from his "infantry ears" and was able turn the volume down enough so it wasn't a nuisance. Unlike my night punctuated with "lullaby by seagull," he reassured me with a self-satisfied grin that he had slept well.

Years later, General Powell took great delight in a speech he gave to an international hotel conglomerate about all the things they do wrong. His list included their preference for using high tech stereo systems with built in alarm clocks that require an engineering degree to operate, having electrical outlets in places that require older-than-middle-aged folk to bend in ways that they otherwise avoid, and having itty-bitty bottles with itty-bitty writing on them in the shower that require glasses to be read—and who wears glasses to the shower?

The hotel executives loved it and were splitting their sides with laughter as they nodded in recognition of his litany of complaints.

Once General Powell retired from the military and was no longer in uniform, he was introduced to and embraced by Martin Greenfield, of Martin Greenfield Clothiers, based in Brooklyn, NY. A Holocaust survivor born in Ukraine, Martin immigrated to the U.S. in 1947 and over the decades became a renowned master tailor, often described as the best men's tailor in the United States. General Powell quickly became a devoted customer and friend, and always joked that he would never dare to appear in anything other than "a Martin suit" anywhere press photographers might be, as Martin's discerning eye could pick up even an eighth of an inch difference in a buttonhole and would surely call to scold. (This is not an exaggeration, as I know it happened more than once.)

But even the best made clothing will eventually show the wear and tear of constant travel. Once, after a series of acrobatic entrances and exits from planes and cars, the General's slacks caught on something and the seam split. With no time in the schedule to change, I was assigned blocking duty whenever we had to move from place to place. In contrast to my usual position, close but *not* hovering, this time I was practically glued to his back. Though we laughed about it afterwards, we did our best throughout the event to keep this sartorial mishap undetected by the masses and the press.

Contrast that wardrobe malfunction with one several weeks later. We were in a private plane traveling between events several states apart. It was early in the morning and when the plane banked the sun came streaming through the windows, and I noticed the weave of the General's exquisitely tailored suit jacket didn't match his slacks.

I am a believer in the old "spinach in the teeth vs. run in the stockings" rule: If it is something that can be easily fixed (i.e., spinach or lipstick on teeth), tell the person. If it is something that cannot be fixed on the spot (i.e., a run in your stockings or a stain on a necktie), it is best to not call attention to it, as this would only embarrass the person. Since the correct jacket and slacks from the mismatched suits were not accessible, this situation was more than spinach in the teeth, so I just smiled to myself and wondered if he would notice. It did not take more than a few minutes before he did and he caught my eye.

Oh, the fun of catching him in an "oops."

* * *

Early in my career, I had the good luck of working many months of the year in Normandy, France. I shared previously that although I can speak some French, I am definitely not fluent.

As General Powell often liked to remind me, I am also not fluent in "car," and cannot carry on an intelligent conversation about anything automobile-related, even in English. So you can imagine what it was like to learn how to drive a stick-shift car in France. I had just arrived in my little town on the Norman coast, suffering from tremendous jet lag with the sun setting on a cold winter night, and my sweet rental-car owners proceeded to give me a ten-minute driving lesson (literally only ten minutes) in French on how to drive a stick-shift car, ending with their final reassurance, "Don't worry—you'll feel it when you need to shift gears."

And then they left me. In the dark. With a car with no power steering and no power brakes. All alone to navigate narrow country roads. Through the miles and miles of countryside before the next village with lights and, eventually, my house.

Driving that car for the first time was terrifying. Remember, this is when neither GPS nor cell phones were prevalent. Traveling those lonely roads in a car I could barely keep going, without another soul in sight, had my nerves on edge. Miraculously, I got through the ordeal with a combination of fervent prayer, tears, and singing Broadway show tunes. As I made my way across the dark, unfamiliar back roads of rural Normandy, I reminded myself that the sun would rise the next day no matter how badly I ground the gears or stalled out.

I tell this story about my perilous driving in foreign lands because it reminds me of General Powell's famous quote, "It ain't as bad as you think. It will look better in the morning."

As much as I was never a car person, he certainly was. He loved cars and delighted in fancy ones. Even though as Secretary of State he had an official driver, the fabulous Otis Pearson from Diplomatic Security, he still had a garage full of cars—among the fancy ones a royal blue PT Cruiser, which I thought looked like a hearse, and an old '66 Volvo station wagon that smelled bad and barely ran.

I learned early on that as much as he was a car guy, he was a terrible backseat driver. He liked to honk my horn, play with my radio, give directions, and tell me to drive faster. After driving him somewhere exactly twice, I simply—and happily—gave him my keys whenever he needed a ride ever after. More often than not, if we had a local event to attend, he would insist on driving his treasured Corvette. The fastest I have ever gone in a car was with him driving it on the Dulles Access Road. (Thank goodness we did not get pulled over!)

Though we teased about our mismatched car appreciation, I always relied on him whenever I needed a new car. He had a dear friend from California in the car business, Steve Reich, affectionately known to me as Steve-the-car-guy, who gladly and generously shared his expertise. When it was time to put my old green Honda (which the General referred to as "an old lady car") out to pasture, during our tenure at the State Department, General Powell connected me with Steve for help. Although the General could not relate to my non-car interest, he certainly respected it.

Alas, poor Steve could not believe how clueless and disinterested I was in identifying even basic preferences in a car other than color. He finally quit communicating with me directly and made the General—the Secretary of State at the time—the go-between for my car selection. I have always been intimidated by car salesmen, so when it came time to go to Steve's chosen dealership to buy and pick up the car (and every car since then), I would bring General Powell along so I could figuratively (if not literally) hide behind him. He would act as my interpreter and negotiator. In the end, thanks to Steve and the General, all I had to do was pay for the car and it was mine.

No one is immune to the occasional flat tire. In the early days together, General Powell did a series of community events in California where I did not accompany him, as they seemed straightforward and I could easily monitor them from afar. I was more than a little upset one day during that trip when I got his call from the side of a major freeway saying his hired car had blown out a tire and, because his driver was elderly, he was going to change the tire himself. Despite my frantic attempts to talk him out of it, the General did indeed change it and, since it was on the driver's side, remained perilously close to traffic. All I could do was call and tell the client the General would be late and make sure she had some industrial soap waiting for him backstage. Once he'd arrived, the General delighted in showing off the grease stains up and down his shirt sleeves to the audience, and relished the telling of every exaggerated moment spent risking life and limb with every pass of a speeding car on the California freeway. The audience loved it.

He was ever the showman.

Years later, while in Trinidad and Tobago, we stopped to hear a local steel drum band play just before heading to the airport for our flight home. The General was in the car of the country's President and I was in the First Lady's immediately behind them. While still two blocks away, our car came to a dramatic stop with a blowout, so the First Lady and I ran the remaining blocks. In the heat and high heels.

Early in my career while en route to Andrews Air Force Base for a diplomat's arrival, I had a blowout during morning rush hour traffic on the Washington Beltway crossing the Woodrow Wilson Bridge. It was a terrifying experience, but I was rescued by a Good Samaritan who stopped, changed my tire, and, after he finished, simply charged me to do something nice for someone else that day. Fast forward to January 2019 when General Powell had a flat tire on the Washington Beltway. He was going to a doctor's appointment at Walter Reed National Military Medical Center, and when his tire blew, Anthony "Tony" Maggert, a fellow veteran, also on his way to Walter Reed, stopped to help. Once Tony posted the selfie taken on the side of the road and it went viral, the national news picked up the story, sharing with the world the General's message, "Thanks, Anthony. You touched my soul and reminded me about what this country is all about and why it is so great. Let's stop screaming at each other. Let's just take care of each other. You made my day."

One final flat tire story. In the days immediately following

General Powell's death and for the next couple months, eight cars of family and friends had flat tires traveling the neighborhood blocks and roads surrounding the Powell residence in McLean. Not that anyone would wish a flat tire on anyone else, but it made us all smile with thoughts of him. With me being the non-car person I am, the fact that my car was seemingly the only one spared… I can't help but smile thinking perhaps I had the benefit of a guardian angel who understood.

* * *

For anyone who has not had the opportunity to be involved in the theater, either as a child in school or as an adult in community theater, I recommend looking for an opportunity. Even if you do not feel called to perform and embrace the "smell of the grease paint, the roar of the crowd" (an oft quoted phrase from the British musical of that title), signing up to be a part of the backstage crew will help you understand the philosophy, "The show must go on!"

This expression likely originated with 19th century circuses. In those days, the show had to keep going to prevent an audience from panicking when a wild animal escaped or a performer became injured.

Fortunately, while on the speaking circuit we never had to battle rampaging wild animals, nor deal with any catastrophic injury in front of crowds (wardrobe misadventures don't count), but sometimes the General's show had to go on in even the worst conditions.

A cardinal rule of travel is never to take the last available scheduled plane. If we were able to charter a private plane, we were in good hands, traveling via Moby Dick Airways with Roy

Oakley or, previously, with Dug Garrett, and we had more control of our schedules. Relying on commercial flights, however, required a more flexible schedule. I always scheduled our travel along with a backup plane, should the scheduled flight be canceled or delayed due to mechanical or weather issues.

Even so, weather is a constant worry on the speaking circuit. During 2010, much of the east coast experienced what came to be known as "Snowmageddon." General Powell was scheduled to give a keynote speech to a trade association at its annual convention in Atlanta. Winter weather watches quickly turned into warnings as blizzards forced the area airports to cancel all incoming and outgoing flights. General Powell's participation in the conference was at risk, as was his attendance at a board meeting in California immediately following. Although all flights out of Washington, D.C. were canceled, Atlanta airports were still open, and he would be able to fly to California if he could first just get to Atlanta.

Once we learned the convention would still proceed despite some members being unable to attend, the General decided to drive. My task was to find an open rental car outlet in Northern Virginia where he could rent a car (driving the treasured 'Vette was unthinkable in blizzard conditions), even though most of them had already closed due to the weather. I finally found a tiny one run out of a local hotel a few miles from the General's home, though the poor gentleman who answered the phone was closing even as we were talking. While keeping him on the line, I had the General on a phone in my other ear and was explaining to him that a car would be waiting if he could get there in the next ten minutes. Luckily, with the masterful help of the Powells' houseman, Frank Branch, the General grabbed the last available rental car and set off through a blinding snowstorm to fulfill his obligation multiple states away.

Over our years together, the General affectionately ordained me his official Mama Bear and babysitter, as I was prone to worry constantly about his security and safety. With this in mind, you can guess how his driving in these risky conditions made me sick with worry. His one concession to me for making this snowy pilgrimage was his promise he would check in periodically and drive very carefully and very *slowly* (something that was hard for him to do). I stayed glued to my phone as I waited for his calls. Each time he called, his laugh and the lilt of his voice clearly told me of his delight in defeating the weather demons on his way to his commitment.

When he finally (finally!) arrived in Atlanta, he was given a hero's welcome by his hosts who bemoaned the absence of the majority of East Coast invitees and some of their other speakers due to the weather. They were shocked by the effort he'd made to get there.

My long hours of worry over his adventure were repaid however, with the chortle of glee and twinkle in his eye every time the General or I told the story thereafter of how he'd braved life and limb in blinding snowstorms to keep a promise.

* * *

There is a 16th century Dutch phrase, "*in de pekel zitten*," or what in English is known as "being in a pickle." This traditionally means being in a difficult situation. It was first used in English by Shakespeare in *The Tempest*.

I was in a pickle with my beloved General during a trip to Miami where he was to be an honored guest of an international investment bank and participate in a panel discussion joining two former prime ministers and the former director of an economic council. In the audience were other former world and national leaders and although this investment bank did not have a protocol staff by title, it had a fabulous team of professionals well-schooled in handling the details of dealing with dignitaries.

My "pickle" in this particular instance was that General Powell had injured his back in a fall earlier that week and was in a lot of pain. To their credit, the event team choreographed how all the panelists would ascend and descend the stage to mask the General's discomfort from the audience. However, upon our arrival in Miami the day before (on my birthday), he fell again at the airport, aggravating his injured back still further. While the panel discussion took place at our hotel, I worried over how best to return to the airport to catch our flight home as worry- and pain-free as I could. Anyone who has ever traveled while sick or in pain knows how challenging it is to get through airport terminals and crowds. Like a raincloud disappearing when the sun suddenly shines through, my concerns eased once I reached out to my friend, Desmond Alufohai, Director of Protocol and International Affairs at the Miami International Airport, who provided his team of miracle workers to help us literally every step of the way. No doubt their efforts would have been extended to anyone in need, but I consider them angels for what they did for us.

As I said earlier, our goal was to maximize what we accomplished on the road so we could minimize time away from home, which often made scheduling complicated. On one trip, we traveled for events in Boise, Seoul, and Tokyo, and only spent two nights in hotels and were back home after just four days! He usually slept well on planes en route to our events while I was always fretting about the logistics upon arrival and so rarely slept at all. By contrast, I would enjoy exhausted sleep on flights home and he would be alert, eager to resume normal life.

My very first helicopter ride was early in my career as part of an observer delegation in El Salvador and, though a mere staffer on the trip, I well remember being less than comfortable seated in one of the outward facing gunner seats (of course unarmed at the time) of a combat helicopter, watching tracer bullets whiz by my feet. As General Powell had been involved in two helicopter crashes during his military career and after, I'm not disappointed we rarely needed to fly in one.

Whenever an event was held in New York City, we quickly confirmed travel by train, as the reliability of Acela and Amtrak was preferable to airport shuttles. Plus, being met at Penn Station by Steve Betancourt's Century II drivers was far easier than being met at LaGuardia Airport, as we were far closer to whatever hotel or event site we were using. Also, for some reason people traveling by train were far less likely to bug the General than crowds in airports. On more than one occasion at the airport, I'd done my best to intimidate an overeager fan who was waving a camera phone and trying to follow the General into a men's room something that never happened at a train station.

Being on the road, in and out of hotels, and on planes, trains, and automobiles was always an adventure. But there really is no place like home, and it was always a pleasure to see the General's eyes light up when we entered his driveway at the end of any trip bringing him back home to Mrs. Powell.

6.

Protocol, Policy, and Precedence

"Check small things."
—Colin Powell

General Powell's Thirteen Rules were first made famous by *Parade* magazine decades ago in 1989. Wherever he went, he was asked about them. Despite the publication's label, he would explain they were not really rules, but rather succinct sayings that were noteworthy for their simplicity. Even so, he wrote about them in both his autobiography, *My American Journey*, and his book on leadership, *It Worked for Me.* The rules were printed on bookmarks we freely shared with client groups or anyone who asked for one, and clients often reproduced them at event giveaways. Somehow, these rules took on a life of their own, appearing in PowerPoint presentations and lectures given by anyone from military leaders to professors.

Of these rules, "Check small things," may be my favorite, as it was tremendously relevant to our daily work. Whether preparing for and attending events on the speaking circuit, or advancing international diplomacy while at the State Department, every little detail mattered. Always.

With a career in the military, General Powell was well versed in protocol long before he was named Secretary of State. He knew that following the formal procedures and etiquette of diplomacy strengthened relationships between disparate countries and organizations.

I remember times when our movements, like any well-rehearsed choreography, determined the outcome of diplomatic efforts.

During our days in New York surrounding the Opening of the United Nations General Assembly (UNGA) each fall, I often served as an official greeter to chiefs of state for their bilateral meetings with Secretary Powell. I would escort one leader into a meeting and as soon as the doors shut, would race (in high heels, mind you), down the hall to greet the next for his meeting immediately following. Although this rotating door of dignitaries was exhausting, it was a typical workday at UNGA.

Usually, heads of delegations could pass one another in hallways, waiting areas, or by motorcade without incident. This was not the case the day we had back-to-back meetings with leaders representing two delegations at war with each another for generations. One of them was Yasser Arafat, President of the Palestinian National Authority.

The two leaders could in no way be seen together, so we mapped an alternate route for President Arafat to avoid them crossing paths. The same courtesies were extended to both leaders and delegations to avoid the possible repercussions should the leaders be seen (or worse yet, photographed) together. Thus, the important matters discussed with Secretary Powell were not overshadowed by unwanted publicity.

Masters of seating charts relish telling stories of manipulating seating arrangements at meals so special connections can be made (or strengthened) or quiet negotiations could continue outside of official meetings. Or, like my story of the two hostile leaders, we sometimes had to seat politically sparring guests far from one another much like parents trying to keep misbehaving children apart.

For any seated event, hours are spent devising the seating arrangements and placing the table place cards. Who should sit next to whom? Will the ambassador of this country get along with the ambassador's wife of that country? Will an important deal be cemented if I sit this corporate leader next to this one? And will this leader who has just become a grandfather for the first time appreciate being next to this renowned children's book author? What if I put this world famous (and charming) tenor beside the very shy wife of a newly elected official to put her at ease and perhaps give her some engaging repartee at what otherwise would be just one more official meal?

Seating arrangements are an example of how protocol is both an art and a science. During the visit of one of Europe's most recognizable chiefs of state, when General Powell was President Reagan's National Security Advisor and I was very junior in the Office of Protocol, we were both involved in a dinner held at Georgetown University. As the National Security Advisor, General Powell was one of the highest-ranking guests and thus was seated at the head table. My job as protocol officer was to liaise with all the agencies involved, do a site walk (called "advancing" the event), and work with university officials to ensure all was ready for the arrival of the foreign leader, with tables and place cards properly arranged.

Never underestimate the power of fading into the wallpaper. Prior to the arrival of the official delegation and guests, from my spot in the shadows I noticed a member of the foreign delegation (also there in advance) grab her place card at a "lesser" table and switch it with one at the head table. While doing this, I overheard her explain to her compatriot from the embassy that being seated at the head table was her right since she was the leader's mistress. She did not seem to be at all fazed by the fact that the leader's wife would be seated there, too.

Despite the entertainment her "revised" seating arrangement might have provided, I switched the place cards back as soon as the woman and her friend left the room. Thus, the Jesuits of Georgetown as well as the leaders of both countries were saved from embarrassment. General Powell and I enjoyed laughing about this infamous place card escapade for decades after.

Strict seating arrangements may seem like small things, but they can be ever so important.

Certainly, there are occasions when the rules of protocol—e.g., following strict seating according to the order of precedence—can and should be broken. For instance, if the place of honor is always "to the right" of the host, what should be done when the guest is deaf in the left ear? Consider as examples, the President of the United States, the Chief of Protocol, the Foreign Secretary of the United Kingdom, and the General Manager of the Blair House among others, who were all deaf in one ear. Would proper protocol require two guests to be seated next to each other in strict protocol order if it placed them at a conversational disadvantage? Would it not be kinder and more nurturing to the relationship if they could communicate clearly by being seated outside of traditional precedent order?

If protocol is both an art and a science, the science is in knowing the accepted international rules of conduct and the art is in knowing when and how to break those rules. The General was a master at both.

* * *

General Powell may not have been much of an athlete, but he still knew far more than I did about sports. His friend, the late Charles Wang, while a partial owner of the NY Islanders hockey team, asked General Powell to come up to New York and be the guest celebrity to toss out the ceremonial puck to start the game. With his usual aplomb, the General dropped the puck and the fans in the stands roared their approval. I don't know if any of the players in that game ended up with a hat trick, but I am certain the General knew hockey protocol well enough that he would have thrown something appropriate onto the rink in celebration if a player had scored three goals.

The baseball equivalent of dropping the ceremonial puck is throwing out the first pitch, and General Powell was asked several times by various teams to do so. One time we were in Boston for a series of events, including a meeting with then Massachusetts governor, Mitt Romney, and our visit coincided with a home game of the Boston Red Sox. Ever generous with sharing the spotlight, General Powell had several children from the local Boys & Girls Club of America join him on the pitcher's mound and actually be the ones to throw the ball.

Since I was tucked away in the dugout with the team, my only contribution to the occasion was to wear a red dress. I could only roll my eyes when the General found this attempt to blend in amusing.

Baseball fans know baseball protocol requires everyone to stand up after the sixth inning for the seventh-inning stretch. Had we stayed through the end of the game, General Powell would surely have risen to his feet, leading the "troops" (as he called them) of fans in the stands.

While traveling for a speaking engagement we once had an opportunity to attend a performance of selections from Handel's *Messiah*. The soloist and choir members had exquisitely beautiful voices and were accompanied by period instruments which added a magical quality to the experience. Many of us rose on cue when the first notes of the *Hallelujah Chorus* were heard in Part II of the oratorio. Judging by the number of people delayed in rising it was clear not everyone there knew to stand up for the *Hallelujah Chorus*, a centuries-old tradition some historians believe was started by British King George II (1683–1760).

The hat trick, the seventh-inning stretch, standing for the *Hallelujah Chorus*—each is a tradition recognized and embraced by many yet foreign to others. In all cases though, General Powell knew the appropriate protocol for the occasion.

Preparing him—or anyone—for the moment, required checking the seemingly small things. Imagine the discomfort when everyone around you knows unspoken rules of behavior that you do not. Isn't this how most Americans feel when visiting another country and experiencing another culture for the first time? It is the same for visitors we receive experiencing our country and culture for the first time.

As examples of culturally specific things we had to understand, we knew to keep the soles of our feet on the ground when traveling in the Middle East, and to avoid using white flowers for center pieces when hosting guests from Asia,. If General Powel didn't already know the particular rules of the road for the situation (and he most often did), I would brief him in advance. Recognizing the appropriate cultural behavior at the proper time and place was a gift we could give those around us—whether they were the General's hosts or his guests.

* * *

There is an old English proverb that states, "Necessity is the mother of invention."

Every time we had to devise a contingency plan to fix an immediate problem, precedent was set and became the standard solution to be followed in future, similar situations. An example of precedent becoming policy is the plan we devised for the recurring bilateral meetings between Secretary Powell and the Foreign Minister of China. The setting for these meetings was often in one of the diplomatic reception rooms on the 8th floor of the State Department. As with most bilateral meetings, the delegations were to be equal in number. If the Secretary of State had a total of eight officials on the approved list for the meeting, then his foreign counterpart was to have eight —and only eight—officials as well. Accompanying support staff members (the straphangers) were not invited to attend the meeting itself and would not be allowed into the room.

Unfortunately, one of the first times the two leaders were to meet we learned in advance that the visiting delegation had many more people in the motorcade en route to the State Department, more than would be allowed into the meeting. Even though the official and approved participants would be seated around the table, we feared the support staff would seat themselves in the decorative chairs lining the room—and claim a diplomatic version of "squatters' rights." As "saving face" was a cultural imperative, we knew it would be embarrassing to remove the straphangers from the room once they were seated, so our best option was to keep them from taking a seat at all.

Sometimes the easiest solutions are best. In the end, we simply removed the extra chairs from the room and hid them. (Would that all diplomatic crises could be so easily and elegantly solved!) Even though the additional staff members entered the room, when it was time for the meeting to start it was obvious there were only enough seats for the participants around the table. Since standing for the meeting and sitting on the floor were not options, once the meeting got underway the staff members retreated without embarrassment. Secretary Powell and the Chinese Foreign Minister were able to have a productive lunch meeting, and no one lost face.

Years later on the speaking circuit, General Powell was scheduled to address a delegation of successful entrepreneurs from Beijing visiting Washington, D.C. They were staying at the Mayflower Hotel, one of Washington's loveliest historic downtown hotels, for several days of meetings with various business leaders and local officials before heading off to other U.S. cities for similar gatherings.

As with most events, I arrived onsite early to advance the event, meet with my contact for a walkthrough, and go over anything still needing to be addressed. Although the event itself was not terribly complicated because this foreign delegation was not bilingual, consecutive interpretation was to be provided throughout the program.

Confirming the interpretation and programming was not a problem but trying to figure out why and how the hosts had arranged flags on the stage had us scratching our heads.

Flag protocol for use in official events is quite specific, though not simple, which keeps protocol officers busy. This time the delegation had, in addition to the United States and the Chinese flags, six flags of other countries from different regions around the world arranged in no discernable order. The U.S. flag was in the middle of the display with the Chinese national flag to the left. The combination of other flags seemed unusual, and I could not figure out why they were even there at all. (For those who do not know, flag protocol in the U.S. is to have the American flag at the viewers far left, and every other flag in alphabetical order to the right.)

My delegation contact was thrilled with the arrangements and had worked diligently with the hotel to set everything up per the group's specific instructions. As I had no explanation why the delegation insisted on displaying these particular flags this way, I turned to the hotel official assigned to oversee the event and whispered my questions to her. When she explained the delegation had simply asked for "any six random flags that would add pretty color for pictures," all I could do was fight the urge to jump onto the stage and rearrange everything.

Gentle urging regarding the reorder or removal of flags on the stage was not welcome, so we proceeded with the stage as designed. Fortunately, this was a private event and closed to the media, so we did not fear photos appearing in the press.

At events where General Powell gave the keynote address and attended a separate meal for VIPs, groups often planned (without asking first) for him to deliver additional remarks at the meal. The General was *not* pleased when faced with an "add on" beyond the contract. To alleviate his irritation and still make everyone happy, I would convince the hosts it would be better for him to deliver "toast remarks" rather than the mini-speech they thought they wanted. It might only be semantics, but my rebranding was a bit more palatable to him than the contractual problems created by forcing him to prepare an additional speech on short notice. Luckily, the General was a master at giving gracious and uplifting toasts that honored his hosts and inspired the guests.

Toasts were something we could laugh about after an event. Although it is not kind to judge others, I confess when I am attending an event and toasts are part of the program, I ignore my better angels and listen to the devil on my shoulder. I sit in judgment, waiting to see if the ones toasting or being toasted know the proper rituals. I sigh with relief or visibly cringe when toasts are made, depending on whether they are proposed and received correctly. It is always possible to find someone else in the room who knows the difference as soon as I hear a gasp or see someone cringe at the sight of the guest of honor figuratively patting himself on the back by drinking along with the toast in his honor. Each time this happens, I have to fight the urge to pull the guest of honor aside with a gentle reminder it is never correct to raise one's own glass when being honored. General Powell would catch my eye with a twinkle in his whenever we watched someone downing a glass of bubbly while being toasted.

Part of the official choreography of presenting official guests at the U.S. Department of State prior to a visit with Secretary Powell was to have them sign a beautifully bound leather guest book before being escorted into the Secretary's office.

The signing ceremony by each guest provided a historical record of the visit, of course, but it also allowed a grace period to manage the flow of the event. When a delegation arrived a few minutes early, having the principal spend a few minutes bent over a book in an anteroom could often fill the extra time an early arrival created. Likewise, if Secretary Powell were delayed for any reason, the delay could be masked by this small ceremonial flourish.

After the visit, the staff calligrapher (in our case at that time the talented Jenny Nicholson) would add the guest's official title and date of the meeting to the page. Like guest books at the White

House and the Blair House (the President's Guest House), the State Department's book not only recorded the history of official engagements, but became a work of art.

Over time, General Powell and I became skillful at recognizing events with excellent planning and execution—as well as those that left room for improvement.

Once, on Long Island, General Powell was the keynote speaker at a business association's 90th anniversary luncheon. Although he had spoken at the annual event several times before, this was the first time I had attended. As with all speaking engagements, I spent days, weeks, and sometimes months in communication with my counterpart to confirm logistics and research the group's background, all before writing a detailed briefing paper to make the General "smart" about the event and audience.

The event went well, General Powell did his usual great job, the hosts were tremendously happy with the success of the event, the tickets sold out with standing room only, and the guests were delighted. This time my responsibilities were simply devoted to taking care of the General and coordinating with the hosts, so I was not responsible for the myriad details required to tend the 1,000 guests. Nonetheless, I could not help but notice examples of some basic event planning rules that were followed well and several others that were inadvertently missed. I had to suppress my impulse to jump in and try to lend a helping hand.

The local U.S. Army Recruiting Center provided the color guard, and the ceremony was perfect. The young woman from a local university who sang the National Anthem had an exquisitely beautiful singing voice, although, in light of her talent, the embellishments to the anthem were not necessary.

Furthermore, guests do not want or need multiple speakers

at a luncheon and there is no need to introduce the introducers. The lead up to the "main course" (so to speak) of speakers should be kept to a minimum. These guidelines were jettisoned at this event quickly however, when a sitting national politician up for reelection chose to attend and wanted to speak, promising "only two minutes." Unfortunately, when up for reelection, it is not in the DNA of any politician to speak for only two minutes on any topic of any sort.

The pervasiveness of social media these days means anything said or done can be—and likely will be—caught on camera and posted immediately on the internet and seen around the world. In other words, the comment or action "grows legs." On a positive note, if ever General Powell had a message he wanted or needed to get out quickly, he knew it only took one camera phone or email. To anything we did on the road I would give a mental "NY Times headline and momma" check: "Would it be something we would want to appear as a headline or something my mother (or even more so, Mrs. Powell) would want to hear or read?

At the event above, the second the General responded to a question asking how he would vote in the upcoming presidential election, one tweet from a guest in the audience made his answer instantaneous news around the world. By the time General Powell finished on stage and we were in the car on the way back to the airport, both our phones were ringing with multiple calls and my email inbox was inundated with Google Alerts showing the breadth and reach of the Twitter comment announcing to the world how he would vote.

It is also good to remember that once something is captured on social media, there is no telling when it will appear again. Remember, my role was to stay in the background whenever possible. If I were doing my job properly, I would always be either just outside the edge of the photo or blending in with the scenery. Because General Powell made instant news with that simple tweet, television news organizations pulled old b-roll footage to run with it. The morning after this event while in line to get coffee, one of my favorite baristas at my local Starbucks announced she had seen me on the news the night before. After she described what I was wearing and the background in the picture, I figured out the footage had been taken in a foreign country several years prior. And, I am relieved to say, I was indeed in the background blending in.

For me, this event also had a funny personal component to it. As always, to make the General "smart," I spent time researching the VIPs who would attend and provided little biographies on many. This information always gave General Powell an edge and with a twinkle in his eye, he would use the information as an "in" to engage his audience. In doing this pre-event legwork for the lunch event though, I stumbled upon the name of a state-elected official that made me take a second look. Although it was a common name, with a quick Google search I discovered the name belonged to someone I had known as a teenager. The minute I confirmed his identity, I hammered out an email to General Powell (in all caps) explaining that this local politician, in addition to his having a very important elected title, had been the-love-of-my-little-college-girl heart. The General teased me relentlessly of course, but he also very sweetly during the VIP photo-op receiving line made a point of connecting with the heartthrob of my youth as soon as they were introduced. General Powell not only engaged him in the receiving line at length but also included him in a shout-out he gave to the U.S. Senator in attendance during the luncheon presentation.

Every small detail does indeed count.

* * *

Modern technology is a wondrous thing, and social media can be a fabulous communications tool that brings us together with words and pictures—when shared correctly.

I accompanied General Powell on visits to several developing countries and fell in love with many of the different cultures we encountered. On one trip, we met a delightful group of young children playing in a mud puddle in front of a hut in a small village. The children were laughing and calling out for us to join them. Imagine the General's and my horror when one of our American escorts pulled out a camera to capture their joyful faces on film, only to find these children suddenly freeze, and their laughter turn to cries of fear as they waved us away. Our escort was unaware the local culture believed that having your picture taken allowed someone to steal a part of your soul. This was a sad and painful reminder that when dealing with people from different cultures and traditions, one should never make assumptions.

I am a Cold War baby. I grew up in a suburb of Washington, D.C., surrounded by oodles of neighbors and parents of friends who all worked for either the military or the many government agencies spread throughout the region. Somehow, we all knew the not-so-secret rumors of what restaurants were known to be KGB hangouts, and even in which apartment complexes spies were rumored to be living. We all devoured Robert Ludlum and John le Carré novels and hurried to our local movie theaters whenever Hollywood's latest spy thriller was released.

With all this as a backdrop, it shouldn't be a surprise to know that whenever traveling in far-flung corners of the world, it was second nature to be a bit clandestine in communications. When in cars, conversations were kept to discussions of the program details of the day or superficial topics, and if not were otherwise in code. When calling each other from hotel phones, General Powell and I were masters of cryptic communication. Why speak paragraphs when often only a few words were necessary? And it never hurt to assume others might be listening or communication lines might be crossed. Even though out of public office, General Powell was a likely target for intelligence operatives.

Once while preparing for an evening event in Guatemala, I was waiting for my contact to call me with updates. When my cell phone finally rang, I was surprised to find the cell phone screen was unreadable—or at least unreadable to me, as the caller ID was displayed in Cyrillic letters. Although I'd still remembered a few words in Russian that I learned as a teenager at a Governors School summer program in Virginia, I'd never learned how to read Cyrillic. My Guatemalan contact and I had spoken many times by phone, so I knew this call was not from her and it certainly was not from General Powell. How and why would my American-purchased mobile phone (which I never let out of my possession) register a caller calling from a Slavic region?

With a cautious "Hello," I answered the call and immediately recognized the caller's voice as one of the General's daughters— who was calling me from New York.

There may have been a mundane explanation for the strange routing of the telephone connection. Then again, perhaps it was simply a good reminder to always be mindful. You never know who may be listening.

It was hard to believe how many tasks I could accomplish

in one day towards the end of my career, tasks that would have taken days back when I was just starting out in the 1980s. Long gone are my days working at an electric typewriter with carbon paper to produce a document in triplicate. Likewise, thanks to modern technology, cables from the State Department to foreign posts are no longer sent via pneumatic tube. (I remember sending cables that way, and I still have no idea why or how the process worked.)

One of my favorite duties while at the State Department was to officiate the swearing-in ceremonies of new ambassadors and senior officials. These ceremonies were tremendously important to General Powell as Secretary of State, as they allowed him to bless and launch his diplomatic "troops" to their next posting with their family and friends present. Before every swearing-in ceremony, I was the official at the microphone as emcee, diplomatically reminding all assembled to "please silence all cellphones, pagers, cameras, watches and anything else that might make noise and be disruptive to the ceremony about to commence." Requesting the silencing of everything capable of making noise was meant as a gentle reminder to be courteous during an important ceremony. One would hope that most people would know to do this without the reminder. Hope is the operative word. Inevitably, despite my cajoling, there was always at least one unwanted and obnoxious sound coming from a high-ranking official who had either ignored me or forgotten to do as requested.

Many years ago, a former colleague told me that in her opinion all government jobs were one of two types: those focused on policy, or those focused on protocol. From the disdain in her voice, I could tell she thought protocol positions were not nearly as important as the policy jobs she'd chosen. She never seemed to understand that in government as well as in so many other areas, they are equally important for success.

While I chose not to challenge her, the gleam in my eye probably betrayed my amusement. I always took great pride in working hard, mostly behind the scenes though sometimes in the spotlight—problem solving, building relationships, and setting precedent. I never questioned the General's mantra to check small things, or doubted that our efforts made a difference.

7.

Diplomatic Affairs

"It showed them that if I trusted them, they could trust me."
—Colin Powell

On March, 29, 2004, the North Atlantic Treaty Organization (NATO) was enlarged by the addition of Bulgaria, Estonia, Latvia, Lithuania, Romania, Slovakia, and Slovenia. These seven Central and Eastern European countries joined NATO following their initial invitation during the 2002 Prague Summit. At 1:00 pm EST, the Prime Ministers of the seven countries handed over their Instruments of Accession to the North Atlantic Treaty Organization to U.S. Secretary of State Colin Powell, who accepted them on behalf of the United States, the depository nation for the Treaty.

My colleagues in the Office of the U.S. Chief of Protocol worked almost around-the-clock for several days preparing for this globally significant occasion. The two major protocol concerns consisted of the arrival of the respective Heads of Government, which would be taken care of by the protocol officers of the Visits division; and the ceremony and lunch, which would be taken care of by the Ceremonials team, of which I was in charge. The lunch was held in the beautiful historic Treasury Cash Room of the

Department of the Treasury. Following the lunch and ceremony, there was a reception on the South Lawn of the White House with the President, but the official procedures for the expansion of NATO were performed through the office of the Secretary of State.

I had been working for General Powell for many years by this time, so as Assistant Chief of Protocol for Ceremonials I prepared him as I always did before a big event, meticulously briefing him both verbally in person and in writing by email the night before, preparing him for the procedure he would need to follow for this historic event to go smoothly. The choreography for the formal ceremony was tremendously complicated, as each prime minister would be announced and invited onto the stage in reverse order of precedence but then be announced in proper order to present the documents to the Secretary. Although I'd briefed him on the plan in great detail, I confirmed the U.S. Chief of Protocol would be the one to brief the prime ministers backstage on their respective roles just before the ceremony started.

The next day all seven prime ministers assembled backstage right on time while their delegations were escorted to their seats. Once the Secretary had greeted everyone, he turned the floor over to the Chief of Protocol to give the stage directions to the prime ministers. To my surprise though, the Chief of Protocol announced that I would be the one to give the "marching orders." I certainly did not see that coming, but I jumped in as if it had been the plan all along and went down the line explaining to each Prime Minister the procedure to follow in order to join the Secretary of State on stage. Out of breath by the time I got to the seventh, one of them announced with a laugh, "Now! Let's see just how fast she can say it all again!" Everyone laughed, even the one prime minister who needed an interpreter; and as the ceremony began, I raced to the foot of the stage on the other side of the curtain so I could be in place to prompt with hand gestures if necessary.

One by one, each head of government presented the Instrument of Accession to Secretary Powell on behalf of each respective government. Once the prime ministers were back at their assigned spots on stage, one gave me a subtle thumbs up, two gave me a smile, and one even gave a smile and a wink.

Best of all though was the nod accompanying the twinkle in the Secretary's eye which said, "Well done." I had helped make the boss look good and, like the proverbial swan, I had kept my desperate paddling underneath the surface of the water out of sight while doing so.

As Secretary of State, General Powell was devoted to the department employees under his care. They may not all have worn military uniforms but they all were still his "troops," and his dedication to their wellbeing was felt throughout the building and among our embassies and consulates overseas. Many of his initiatives and programs for their benefit are still in place today. When he changed what had always been known as Foreign Service Day to Foreign Affairs Day, he indicated his support of *all* Department of State employees, not just those in the Foreign Service. As he often said, even as a chapter title in his book, *It Worked for Me*, for anyone who ever worked with him it was always "one team, one fight."

Ever the diplomat, Secretary Powell was well respected by members of the Diplomatic Corps in Washington, D.C. The credentialing of foreign diplomats as their country's representative to the United States involves presenting credentials to the Secretary of State before a subsequent ceremony for presenting the credentials to the President at the White House. Even though the meeting followed a formal procedure, Secretary Powell always warmly welcomed the diplomat, recognizing the new ambassador's responsibility on behalf of his or her country. He always closed their meetings by saying he looked forward to working together to build mutual trust between our respective nations.

Although he had many occasions to interact with foreign ambassadors during individual meetings and visits of government leaders, Secretary Powell delighted in welcoming the entire diplomatic corps with their spouses to the State Department for our annual Independence Day celebration. There is no better view of the Fourth of July fireworks than from the 8th-floor balcony of the State Department, so it was a gift to share the display with the diplomats from this vantage point. For the four years the General was Secretary, we had great fun creating a fabulous red, white, and blue evening serving classic American regional specialties. To top off the evening, the Military District of Washington provided musical entertainment by playing an assortment of patriotic and traditional music, as well as show tunes from Broadway.

Secretary Powell even dressed the part—replacing a diplomat's unofficial coat and tie uniform with what he termed his Thomas Jefferson shirt (known by me as his pirate shirt) and khakis. With Mrs. Powell at his side, he welcomed everyone with a receiving line and later delivered brief welcome remarks with a toast. The rest of the evening was spent mixing and mingling while sharing our national day with representatives from around the world. Without a doubt, these celebrations were joyful.

Although posing for a selfie or a group shot was not something he enjoyed in private life, when the ambassadors whipped out their cameras and phones on these occasions it was somehow ok. Inevitably, at some point in the evening, all the female ambassadors would gather around Secretary Powell demanding their annual group photo. With more ambassadors being male than female, this gathering of the women was always a point of pride for them.

One of the women ambassadors I came to know exceptionally well was the ambassador from Bulgaria. I had been the one to accompany and introduce her to the Secretary and the President when she presented her credentials as ambassador. Tall and elegant, in her observations of what it was like to be an ambassador in Washington, D.C., she was also always gracious and enthusiastic in sharing about her country as well. At one of the receptions she attended, she was asked what had surprised her most when she'd first moved to Washington, D.C.. Her face lit up as she told a story of her earliest days as an ambassador. As a newcomer to the city, she'd puzzled over why the sidewalks at every street corner near the embassy seemed to be "broken." Her embassy was located in a particularly lovely part of town, so it seemed odd to her that every sidewalk had a defect at the street corner where breaks in the cement had been replaced with sloped sections containing tiles with raised ridges and patterns. She was relieved when she learned the "broken" sidewalks were designed to provide ease for wheelchairs and visually impaired pedestrians. It was impossible not to share her joy in discovering that what she had initially perceived as damage was a kind accommodation for those who needed it.

What a wonderful reminder that there is often more than one way of looking at something.

*   *   *

Like most of us, General Powell—and certainly Secretary Powell—was never fond of red tape. He was also not fond of superfluous bureaucratic restrictions or regulations. To him, if something could be simplified, it should be. If bureaucratic speak could be clarified, it needed to be.

One of his favorite stories on the speaking circuit was that of having tasked two Foreign Service officers with briefing President George W. Bush for his first bilateral meeting with his Mexican counterpart, President Vicente Fox. Standard operating procedure at the State Department had always been for senior level officials—say, the Assistant or Deputy Assistant Secretary of the region—to do the presidential briefings and always with official PowerPoint presentations as visual aids. Secretary Powell wanted none of that. Instead, he wanted the two junior desk officers to do the briefing, completely without the "crutch" of slides. No dog and pony show. No red tape. Just two young professionals educating the President of the United States on all he needed to know to prepare for the meeting with President Fox.

As General Powell liked to tell the story, the fact that he trusted these young junior Foreign Service officers to do the briefing with the President became instant news within the Department of State. The news spread like wildfire through the building that the Secretary of State trusted everyone in the department—down to the most junior officials—to do their jobs and to rise to the occasion, even to the point of briefing the President. "And you know what?" General Powell emphasized. "It showed them that if I trusted them, they could trust me."

Shortly after leaving the Department of State, I attended a reception and panel discussion on "Culture, Career & Conversation" at the Embassy of the Kingdom of Bahrain. Part of the panel discussion focused on the importance of international relations and promoting international business. Welcoming international business investment is such a priority for the Bahraini government that the motto of Bahrain's Investors' Centre was "Red Carpet, Not Red Tape!"

Whether it was the military, State Department, or private industry, General Powell was a veteran in navigating bureaucracies. Regulations that may have been put in place for good reasons, taken to an extreme, can complicate plans by requiring levels of approval and analysis far beyond what is necessary. Despite the ever-present and annoyingly unavoidable red tape of bureaucracy, "red carpet treatment"—i.e., "ceremonial courtesy"—made the hassle of dealing with regulations easier to tolerate.

* * *

Among the many awe-inspiring memorials found around the National Mall in Washington, D.C. is the impressive Martin Luther King, Jr. Memorial. Dedicated in 2011, this memorial features a breathtaking 30-foot sculpture of the revered leader of the American Civil Rights movement. The sculpture is a stunning and impressive likeness of Dr. King, depicting him as if he has emerged from the granite behind him and is gazing into the horizon.

The very first time I saw a picture of the statue I was certain the artist was Chinese. And yes, the sculptor is the gifted Chinese artist, Master Lei Yixin. Although I have a background in art and part of my deduction was due to academic study, I was equally informed by experience.

Over his career, General Powell often received portraits as gifts from distinguished visitors—some of which were even hung in the hot tub room next to his basement home office, in the Bunker. Each painting was at least a recognizable likeness of him, and we had fun bringing visitors into the room and letting them identify which portrait came from Romania, Egypt, Japan, or the NAACP. Without fail, guests could correctly identify the origins. As General Powell would point out, the one from Romania made him look a bit like Dracula, the one from Egypt a bit like a sheik, the one from Japan had eyes with slight epicanthic folds, and the one from the NAACP depicted him with a slightly darker skin tone.

We see the world through our own eyes. We can't help it. To some degree, we all see the world with a cultural bias.

In an article that stayed with me long after I read it, Dominican Sister Lucianne Siers, the director of the Institute of Religious Formation at the Catholic Theological Union in Chicago, wrote of "interculturality"—that is, how to embrace the dimensions of many cultures rather than turning everything into a monoculture. Much like what I learned in seventh grade Social Studies class as the "salad bowl" vs. the "melting pot" theory, Sister Lucianne Siers' explained interculturality as being like "a burst of fireworks that have just many, many different colors."

Indeed, from all corners of the world, each culture and experience can be brighter and more colorful than the last.

Over the years, General Powell had many speaking engagements in South Korea as a guest of his friend, Poongsan Corporation CEO Jin Roy Ryu. Audiences were sometimes business leaders and other times university students or cadets at the Korea Military Academy in Seoul (an equivalent of our U.S. Military Academy at West Point). In addition to the official events, Roy hosted many informal VIP dinners, and invited to most of them a South Korean singer named Kim In-soon. Known as Insooni, she shared a birthday with General Powell (April 5th) and also a love of R&B music. Whenever they were together, at some point after sharing a hug they would break out into song and the rest of us could only stand back, watch, and listen in delight.

In preparation for a trip to Asia in September of 1997, I was faced with the challenge of filling the "downtime" between flights from Tokyo to Mumbai, and then from Mumbai to Singapore. I have mentioned the General was never one for shopping or randomly wandering museums, but because of the complicated travel schedule we had more free time than usual on this trip. I provided him with a list of opportunities my client contact had suggested might interest him. As expected, the options of visiting a world-renowned museum or an exclusive shopping district were met by his exaggerated eye roll and a yawn. As soon as I mentioned though a visit to a Sumo Stable where Sumo wrestlers train (accompanied by my own eye roll), General Powell perked up and elatedly proclaimed he'd always wanted to visit a Sumo Stable, and he proceeded to lecture me on the finer points of Sumo wrestling. (I'll admit I hadn't realized there were a multitude of fine points related to what had up till then looked to me like a mere pushing contest between two huge men.)

Soon enough, while killing time before our late-night flight to India, we visited the Sumo Stable and had tea with the world's top Sumo wrestler, Chad "Akebono Tarou" Rowan. In the photograph of us seated on the stable's rush mat, compared to the hulking Sumo champion the over six-foot-tall General looks like a schoolboy and I look like a little doll. The General was as happy as any fanboy meeting a famous athlete could be.

On another occasion, when we had time to kill in a Green

Room at a convention center in Las Vegas, I was tending the needs of two former U.S. Secretaries of State, a former U.S. Ambassador to the United Nations, a former Chairman of the Joint Chiefs of Staff, a former National Security Advisor, a university professor, a refugee, and the authors of six bestselling books. The amazing thing was that all these very influential positions were embodied by just two people who were dear friends of each other: my General and Dr. Madeleine Albright. On this occasion, they were keynote speakers for a fireside chat in front of an audience of several thousand people who were attending a trade association conference.

Usually when staffing such an event, my major responsibility was to shepherd the General and Dr. Albright, along with her aide-de-camp, around the venue throughout the program of events. Being by their sides anticipating their needs before they realized they needed anything could be challenging but I enjoyed my time with them, savoring their shared wisdom and friendship.

While reminiscing about past events and the friendships they had formed over the years with other world leaders, they decided it would be fun to call a mutual friend—their former Russian counterpart, former Foreign Minister Igor Ivanov.

Fortunately, Dr. Albright had his number in her cellphone so with just one punched button they were soon affectionately saying *"Dobryj dyen!"* on speaker to their friend. Their buddy, Igor, was recuperating from recent surgery at a resort thousands of miles away from both Russia and the United States and was understandably surprised to hear the voices of his old friends. More than his happy surprise was his obvious delight in knowing his friends were together and thinking of him.

The call didn't last long but the moment was priceless. Old friends who had shared the world stage—sometimes working together on international agreements, sometimes disagreeing on international challenges, often navigating and representing their respective government's needs in opposition to each other's—were able to enjoy great affection over a simple phone call. Theirs was a bridge of friendship built and developed over the years.

Even as an adult, one of my favorite rides in all Disney theme parks is "It's a Small World," despite the accompanying song playing in my head long after the ride ends. I glory in every opportunity to be reminded of how small the world really is.

Many foreign ambassadors with whom I have worked have risen in the ranks to ministerial positions. The ambassador from Slovenia I escorted for his credentialing ceremonies eventually became Foreign Minister, and two ambassadors I credentialed from Uzbekistan ended up working as, then trading roles as ambassador and Foreign Minister. Of course, it happened even more often for General Powell, and he would encounter someone he had worked with at some point in his storied career almost anywhere we went.

When it was someone who had risen in rank within the foreign ministry, it was always a pleasure to offer congratulations while reminiscing about earlier days. When it was someone against whom the General had worked while in uniform during the Cold War, seeing his warm greeting of an old adversary was remarkable.

Those moments are magical that remind us how small the world is. To encounter someone you have not seen in decades in an unexpected corner of the world is a delightful surprise. Reconnecting with people with whom you have shared significant moments in their careers can be extraordinary.

On that same trip to Guatemala in which my phone bizarrely registered the caller ID in Cyrillic letters, the General and I had one of those memorable small world encounters. General Powell had been invited to deliver a keynote speech to an international gathering of business leaders. Both our housing and the conference were held at a fabulous resort built in and around the ruins of a monastery destroyed by an earthquake several centuries ago. Despite our long hours of travel (including a helicopter ride) and all the official things we had to do while there, the setting was enchanting and the conference hosts delightful, so it felt as if we had been welcomed by longtime friends for a visit instead of just for a work trip.

At an official dinner reception under the moon and stars, we had the unexpected pleasure of seeing the former ambassador to the United States from Guatemala. I had been the protocol officer assigned to escort him to the State Department to present his credentials to Secretary Powell and on a separate occasion I had escorted him by motorcade to the White House for his Oval Office ceremony with President George W. Bush. As we had both moved on to other jobs since then, this was the first time we had seen each other in over a decade. We reconnected as if we had not been separated by years and miles, simply picking up where we'd left off as fond diplomatic colleagues.

I only needed to whisper into the General's ear the reminder that as Secretary of State he had been the first U.S. official to recognize the ambassador in Washington all those years ago; and with that gentle reminder, General Powell worked his magic, greeting the former ambassador as the old friend he indeed was.

For the conference itself, my onsite contact was a woman who worked for the CEO hosting the event, and she was exceptional: gracious, charming, professional and composed, even on the rare occasions when some random detail went amiss. We spent many hours on the phone, exchanged many screens worth of emails in preparation, and, once there, devoted considerable time together for site walkthroughs. During one of these walkthroughs, as I was marveling over and complementing her on the myriad event details she and her team had finessed in this incredible setting, she blurted out, "I just love my country!"

Her delight was infectious and after that exchange everything I saw while there was filtered through her rosy glow. Her simple expression of delight made me realize she was as much an ambassador of her country as the old friend who had officially held the title.

This was always the case with General Powell. Whether attired in a military uniform or business suit, he presented himself well on behalf of whatever organization he was representing at the time.

In this post-9/11 world, most gatherings of the diplomatic corps for official U.S. Government events required ambassadors and chiefs of mission to pass through a security check at the U.S. Department of State before boarding charter buses to the official venue. This usually prevented the ambassadors from having to go through the security at the event site. To make the process as painless and pleasant as possible, protocol officials work hard, providing guidance, refreshments, and hospitality until movement to the final destination. This is an example of the "ceremonial courtesies" I mentioned before, extended to help mitigate discomfort imposed by security and red tape requirements.

In the case of the U.S. Presidential Inauguration, because the swearing-in ceremony of the new U.S. President is with rare exception held on January 20th, the day is often extremely cold. Consequently, even after the Office of the Chief of Protocol's staff has done everything possible to receive members of the Diplomatic Corps with all due respect, the members nonetheless must be in place on the steps of the U.S. Capitol well in advance of the ceremony's start. This often means these distinguished officials sit out in the cold for a long time, unsheltered from wind and sometimes rain or snow, experiencing firsthand the idiom, "hurry up and wait."

In 2005, the day of President George W. Bush's second inauguration ceremony was frigid with snow flurries. As a member of the President's cabinet, Secretary Powell was seated very close to the first family. He was taken to his seat just a short while before the start of the program. In contrast, those of us shepherding the Diplomatic Corps were seated further to the side, although still on the steps of the Capitol, and had been in our seats with the ambassadors for close to an hour already when it started. And it was cold.

However, sharing the ceremony of a peaceful transfer of power with foreign diplomats was a special privilege. The majesty of the occasion somehow overshadowed the discomfort of shivering in the cold.

In contrast, two days later I was on a plane to Kyiv to attend the inauguration ceremony of the new President of Ukraine, Viktor Yushchenko. Secretary Powell was the head of the U.S. Delegation representing President Bush, and I was the senior protocol official assigned to take care of the rest of the delegation. As with our inauguration ceremony just days before in Washington, D.C., Kyiv in January is cold. And like our U.S. inaugurations, the Ukrainian ceremony is held outside. The snow there on this occasion though was substantially more than a few flurries.

As the U.S. delegation, we were seated close to the new president—so close that it was impossible not to notice the disfigurement of his face. During his presidential campaign just months before, one of the world's most potent dioxins had been used in an assassination attempt on his life. Although he survived the poisoning, some of the effects of ingesting the dioxin left his handsome face severely pocked and discolored. Despite the celebratory joy of the ceremony, it was impossible not to be moved by the sobering reminder that the people of Ukraine, like those in many democracies in the world, faced unimaginable challenges.

I returned to Kyiv with General Powell several years later at the request of businessman Viktor Pinchuk that the General give a speech at the Kyiv School of Economics. As this trip did not involve any official government ceremonies, we were free to enjoy the hospitality of the General's host, which included a private tour of the PinchukArtCentre, the largest private contemporary art center in Central and Eastern Europe. Despite the General's usual avoidance of museums while on the road, this was an unusual opportunity, as it included an art installation of fog. As hard as it is to describe, the exhibit actually involved our entering a sealed room containing nothing but fog. Once the door closed behind us, within a foot of entering we were enveloped in fog so intense it was impossible to see the end of your arm much less another person standing beside you. It was so disorienting, in order to not get lost I had to find the General's shoulder blindly and hold on for guidance. Once we'd escaped the fog and eventually left the center, we joined Viktor Pinchuk and his wife for a special private dinner at their dacha just outside the city. Although the menu was a traditional—and delicious—meal of Ukrainian cuisine, it was held in an authentic Japanese teahouse situated in the middle of a large, meticulously maintained Japanese garden, complete with authentic *gongshi* (i.e., scholar stones), shipped over from the Japanese mountains.

The contrast of cultures side by side was incredibly stark, as was the contrast between our earlier visit to Ukraine for the inauguration of the poisoned leader and our return to Kyiv for such unique cultural experiences.

I could always trust that traveling this small world at the side of the General during those many years would forever be eye-opening and remarkable.

8.

Food, Flowers, and Finer Things

"No airborne desserts!"
  —Colin Powell

When General Powell returned to public service as the Secretary of State, I was delighted to accompany him. I returned to the Office of the Chief of Protocol where I'd started my career years ago, but this time as the Assistant Chief of Protocol for Ceremonials and Special Assistant to the Secretary of State. In that role, my staff and I were responsible for all the entertaining Secretary Powell did on behalf of the United States. Whenever he hosted a function honoring a chief of state (e.g., presidents, kings, and queens), head of government (e.g., prime ministers), foreign minister, or member of the diplomatic corps, we managed everything "from the soup to the nuts."

Having been in the Ceremonial Office when George Shultz was the Secretary of State, I remembered events we'd organized when he entertained his foreign counterparts during the Cold War. General Powell and George Shultz had worked well together during the Reagan Administration and were quite fond of each other. As

I prepared for our first event, I reminded General Powell how we'd done things during the Shultz era, giving detailed descriptions of the state luncheons and official dinners we'd hosted. I also shared Secretary Shultz's signature menu choices—especially his preferred dessert: a delicious sorbet wreathed in fresh fruit and accompanied by delicate lace cookies.

Despite my glowing and detailed descriptions, the General responded with a growl, "*Ha! Sorbet is not a dessert! Make my desserts* real *desserts!*"

Thus, I had the enviable task of planning out a menu of cakes, soufflés, mousses, and anything dripping with chocolate.

During Secretary Shultz's tenure, when General Powell was the National Security Advisor and I was a junior protocol officer, I'd learned the dangers of committing a floral faux pas. It was easy to research and confirm which colors and types of flowers were culturally problematic and needed to be avoided. With East Asian cultures, we knew to avoid using white flowers, as they often connote death and mourning. Likewise, carnations and chrysanthemums had funereal connotations so needed to be avoided when working with delegations as varied as France, Germany, Italy, and Japan. Similarly, rather than worrying about which cultures were triskaidekaphobic, we avoided allowing anything in numbers of thirteen. These cultural nuances may seem inconsequential to some. However, being aware of them allowed the hard work of diplomacy to not be derailed by inadvertent offense.

It is equally important to ensure table decorations are not a distraction from negotiations across a table, a lesson I learned during those early years at an official dinner in honor of a foreign leader. I will never forget seeing Secretary Shultz personally remove an offending floral centerpiece because it blocked his view of the guests opposite. General Powell remembered that event as well, so while he was Secretary of State, I made sure he never had to defoliate the head table. To avoid making guests stretch their necks like curious ostriches to see across the table, we gave every tall centerpiece the "sit down test." Before the guests arrived, I'd grab a colleague (or even an innocent bystander) to sit across the table from me with the centerpiece between us and make sure conversation and sight lines were not impeded by the décor.

I was also mindful of the smell test. No matter how beautiful a stargazer lily is, its fragrance does not blend well with the chef's epicurean masterpieces. It can also send guests susceptible to migraines running for the door.

Although the General paid little attention to flowers of any sort, he always assumed we would plan for the comfort of his guests. And we did.

When traveling, he also gracefully accepted gifts of flower bouquets doubtless not knowing a lily from an orchid. In India, for example, he would proudly wear the proffered floral *malas* when they were draped around his neck, but once out of the spotlight, he happily gave each to me, knowing I would get far more enjoyment out of them than he would.

I have always loved formal dinner parties. Whether attending, planning, or organizing one for dignitaries, there is something special about an elegant gathering of people breaking bread together. Somehow all the long hours of preparation are worth it when the guests are spellbound by the magic of the event. The table settings, the place cards, the flowers, the candles, and of course the fabulous menu—these were the trappings of the world I inhabited and helped create for others.

When he became Secretary of State, my Protocol-Ceremonial

Office colleagues and I were delighted to plan Secretary Powell's first dinners honoring his foreign counterparts. The official china and crystal with the Great Seal of the United States engraved or etched in gold on each piece glistened. The flower centerpieces were lovely "long and lows" or beautifully arranged bouquets. And of course, the table linens were exquisite, chosen to compliment the 18th century American antiques displayed throughout the Diplomatic Reception Rooms.

Following one of the smaller of these first special dinners, Secretary Powell called me into his office to discuss the event. I was basking in a warm glow of satisfaction, reflecting on the success of the evening, and was looking forward to his accolades for a job well done. Ah, but as a reminder that one should never pat oneself on the back, what awaited me instead was a very important lesson to avoid in future menu choices:

"Leslie, the dinner was lovely but in the future, no airborne desserts!"

How could that be? The dessert we'd chosen was an exceptionally delicious chocolate confection with a raspberry puree swirl and a scoop of fancy ice cream on the side.

Sigh. It was the ice cream. Unfortunately, no one had thought to check to see if the ice cream might have been *too* frozen. (Who knew ice cream ever could be too frozen?) To hear Secretary Powell tell it, with a twinkle in his eye, the guests chased this hard-as-rock frozen dessert around their plates, brandishing their dessert forks and spoons like hunting spears and, according to the Secretary, at least one poor soul sent the blasted thing flying off his plate and across the table!

A perfect example that every detail is important, no matter how seemingly small.

* * *

In the early days of any new cabinet member's tenure, the members of the civil service who serve from one administration to another spend time getting used to the new incumbent's way of doing business. (As a side note, I tip my hat to those who look beyond the politics of one administration to another and simply do their jobs to the best of their abilities. If only I could make the American public and members of the media recognize and appreciate more the quiet dignity in those who embody the term, "public servant.") My staff—who had all become dear friends—were mostly civil servants, and although many of them knew me from when George Shultz was Secretary, they didn't know General Powell. I suspect they, too, had a bit of the military version of the White Coat Syndrome I'd had when I started working with him, and they were somewhat intimidated by his four-star aura.

On one of my first days on the job, following a meeting with the State Department's financial manager, upon entering my suite of offices I immediately sensed something was wrong. Members of my professional and talented staff were all stumbling over their words trying to tell me that *the* Secretary of State had thrown open the door a bit earlier looking for me.

The fact that the Secretary of State had done this was in and of itself remarkable to them. Our little suite of offices was just off the lobby inside the entrance of the State Department, but the Secretary of State (no matter who) never ever came into these offices.

Of course, this in itself seemed completely normal to me, frankly, no big deal. If he needed or wanted me, I knew Secretary Powell would come looking.

But that wasn't the main thing that had my colleagues so animated.

Once they had told him I was not in, they'd asked what they could do for him in my stead. His response had left them almost incoherent.

That week was his first opportunity to host the lunch of four—"the Cheney, Rummy, Condi, Colin lunch"—which took place monthly. He directed my staff to tell me that he wanted the lunch in the historic James Monroe Room, with the wait staff attired in black tie and the setting as formal as possible—which meant fine china, crystal, linens, and even "those silver dome things." (They are properly called cloches though he would never have used the term.) *Then*, with a straight face, he had explained that he wanted for the menu, "peanut butter and jelly sandwiches on white bread, a bag of chips, a cookie, and the yuckiest drink you can find—maybe that chocolate drink, Yoo-hoo."

Oh, and he'd wanted it all tucked inside little brown bags with each of the four names written on top in magic marker like an elementary school child's lunch. He'd finished his instructions with, "Just tell Leslie. She'll understand."

Secretary Powell could put on his "Four-Star General Face" when he wanted to, as he knew it intimidated those who didn't know him. From the description from my staff, he'd reveled in his full General mode as he described the elegant preparations he wanted for this high-level meeting with the senior members of the administration. I can well imagine my colleagues hanging on his every word, carefully writing down his instructions in order to perfectly meet his expectations, nodding in agreement—all before staring wide-eyed as he dictated the menu and its presentation.

My poor staff was shell-shocked. Not only had *the* Secretary of State barged into our offices, but he had asked them to plan a meal utterly foreign to them. To serve a lunch no better than a kindergartener's to the Vice President, the Secretary of Defense, *and* the National Security Advisor was incomprehensible. Surely, he couldn't be serious?

But I couldn't help but laugh. Once I'd wiped my eyes and caught my breath, I assured them he was quite serious and that we would indeed plan the lunch exactly as he'd described it. I had no difficulty getting the kitchen to prepare the menu Secretary Powell wanted. The hardest part was convincing Jennifer Nicholson, our award-winning and internationally trained calligrapher to sloppily scrawl the names of the guests on the paper sacks so that they looked like they'd been written by the loving but harried mother of a five-year-old. What a joy to introduce my General—with his collegial sense of humor and joy of life—to my staff.

When the day of the lunch came, we had everything prepared. After he'd greeted his guests and all were seated, Diplomatic Rooms Manager Wileva Johnston, beloved butler Jerry Richardson, talented chef Candida Pulupa, and I gathered to stand behind each chair around the table. When the Secretary gave me the wink, I cued the others, and with great synchronized fanfare, we lifted the cloches to reveal the bag lunches.

There was silence as the three stared at the humble brown paper bags before them. Then they all broke into laughter and Vice President Cheney said simply, "Good one, Colin." Eventually my colleagues got used to the Secretary popping into our offices. His private elevator was just feet away, so it was not unusual for him to stop by when he was crossing the lobby. We kept a bowl of candy just inside the door, so I was never sure if he was coming to see us or to satisfy his sweet tooth.

* * *

In planning menus, we always showcased what our chefs did best. There was never a need to serve French food to the French, Chinese food to the Chinese, and so forth. Instead, we would always abide by the known cultural or dietary restrictions of the guest of honor and delegation and plan accordingly.

I had a good relationship with my friend Cathy Fenton, the Social Secretary at the White House, and we would work closely with the Social Office staff to plan complimentary menus for official visits of dignitaries. For a State Visit, no diplomat wants to be served the same menu for lunch at the State Department that is served later for dinner at the White House.

This was an issue General Powell and I had experienced the hard way. On one of his speaking tours through Asia, over the course of a day and a half, we'd been served abalone and sea urchin in three back-to-back meals. Although both were considered cultural delicacies, neither of us would ever have claimed craving either dish. Whenever we reminisced about that trip, we well remembered why I always packed a traveling medicine cabinet. Being prepared for anything was always paramount.

One of the first large official lunches given by Secretary Powell at the beginning of President Bush's administration involved the U.S. Departments of State and Justice and their Mexican counterparts. It was held during a bilateral meeting focused on U.S.-Mexican foreign policy and trade issues. For this lunch, the first course was a fresh seafood mélange arranged artistically to fill and overflow tall stemmed crystal glasses. As it would be pre-plated and pre-set, it would provide a "wow" factor for guests as they entered the room, before they took their seats.

As always, when other U.S. cabinet members were guests to events at the State Department, their advance teams would come early to walk the routes, check the seating, and do anything needed to make their bosses "smart." Since this was normal, it didn't bother us as we scurried around with last minute preparations.

This time however, our well-laid plans were scattered to the winds when one of the advance men pointed out a potential life-and-death concern that should have been raised days earlier. He told us his cabinet member was allergic to shellfish—and could die if he took even one bite.

We were just minutes away from the arrival of the delegations and the first course—resplendent with shellfish—had already been set at each place. This was the early days of President George W. Bush's administration, so perhaps the advance man was new to the job, or his office was newly aware of the allergy. Whatever the case, usually something of this import would have been shared when responding to the invitation, *not* just prior to arrival. Fortunately, he reassured us, the cabinet member could be safely present while others ate shellfish; so we had the wait staff quickly exchange that one place setting of potentially lethal crustaceans for a plain green salad, just in time for the first arrivals.

*   *   *

Knowing what to prepare in advance is not always easy. For a lunch honoring a leader from Saudi Arabia, the embassy informed us that for health reasons the leader was on a liquid diet. We had no problem preparing for this and confirmed with the caterer appropriate liquid first and main courses as well as dessert. We were not prepared, however, after everyone was seated and the first courses were placed, when several other members of the Saudi delegation asked to exchange their lunches for liquid versions as well, in deference to their leader. Luckily, professional caterers always have "extras" at hand.

* * *

It was always a delight to discover a jewel of a place while traveling with the General. One of my favorite examples of this was when we traveled to the Bled Strategic Forum where General Powell was the keynote speaker. I still smile when I think about the beautiful town of Bled, Slovenia, less than an hour from the capital Ljubljana, and of the gracious people we met there.

When the mayor said in his welcome remarks, "As I drove down the Alpine roads to get here and looked around, I couldn't help but thank God for this beautiful world!" it was impossible not to be charmed.

Once again, here was a wonderful small world situation. The Foreign Minister of Slovenia at the time was Samuel Žbogar, a diplomat I had shepherded in 2004 for his White House credentialing ceremonies as ambassador to the United States. I had also been the one to introduce him officially to Secretary Powell.

For the forum, General Powell delivered remarks during the meeting as well as the keynote address at the dinner that evening. Everything about the dinner was spectacular: the ballroom was beautifully decorated with flowers and candles, the tables were perfectly seated, and the keynote speech was exceptional (although I admit I'm biased on that score). It was easy to see that the event planners and government officials had worked long hours to make sure everything was designed to impress the many international guests present. Those in charge had planned a memorable meal of multiple courses prepared by renowned chefs and paired with delicious local wines.

From the time we'd arrived in Ljubljana two days prior to the dinner, we had heard about the famous Lake Bled Cream Cake, *kremna rezina*. It seemed that almost everyone we met, including the president, the foreign minister of Slovenia, and the mayor of Bled, extolled the virtues of this iconic Slovenian dessert. Consequently, when a very elaborate French dessert was presented at the end of the dinner, it was difficult for General Powell and me to mask our disappointment. Sadly, someone considered the Lake Bled Cream Cake too plebeian to serve to this sophisticated international group.

My dear Slovene contact, Ajša Vodnik, Executive Director of the American Chamber of Commerce in Slovenia, saw through our façade, however, and quietly left our table to slip into the kitchen and sweet talk the chef into finding two slices of his *kremna rezina* just for us. The chef initially balked at her suggestion, as he believed the cake would not be as special as the fancier epicurean masterpiece we had already been served.

Nonetheless, when waiters emerged from the kitchen with slices of *kremna rezina* as a surprise just for the two of us, we couldn't contain our joy and our tablemates even applauded in amusement at our reaction.

The cake was absolutely delicious, and my friend Ajša's kitchen detour was a thoughtful gift the General and I greatly appreciated.

Ever since that wonderful dinner, I've tried to remind myself that there is something very special about sharing simple pleasures, fancy doesn't necessarily mean better, and what is traditional or seen as a comfort or even peasant food may be the perfect gift when breaking bread together.

On the rare occasion when Secretary Powell and Mrs. Powell hosted a foreign counterpart in their home, the meal was elegant but simple. Foreign Ministers Joshke Fischer and Igor Ivanov, from Germany and Russia, respectively, were guests on several separate occasions and enjoyed the Powell hospitality without pretention.

* * *

Although we were always quick to adhere to proper protocol, there were times that required bending the rules to meet the problem at hand.

If you have ever enjoyed Baked Alaska, you know it's a delicious pairing of ice cream and cake covered by baked meringue. This iconic dish was created in 1867 at Delmonico's in New York City to recognize the acquisition of Alaska by the United States. To quote Wikipedia's description:

> The dish is made of ice cream placed in a pie dish lined with slices of sponge cake or Christmas pudding and topped with meringue. The dessert is then placed in an extremely hot oven just long enough to firm and caramelize the meringue. The meringue is an effective thermal insulator, and the short cooking time prevents the heat from melting the ice cream.

Serving a dessert that embraces the union of such hot and cold extremes requires precise coordination by the chefs and the wait staff to ensure the guests receive a perfectly prepared serving— before it becomes a dripping, unappetizing mess.

At an event in the Swiss Embassy in Washington, D.C., Embassy Chef Joao Marcos Barboza told the story of serving

Baked Alaska at an embassy dinner for 80 guests. To avoid it melting, he had to get all 80 servings in and out of the oven and then out to each guest in less than two minutes—which was a huge challenge. He quickly realized that dessert needed to be served when ready, even though the ambassador was still at the lectern giving remarks. When the Baked Alaska was ready, it could wait for no one.

Whenever I learned from Secretary Powell that time was tight on a particular day, we would choose soup for a first course—eating soup with a spoon is far faster than eating a salad with a fork. Likewise, we would plan fish for a main course knowing a fish knife is speedier than the utensils required for beef, lamb or chicken.

Usually, simple is better.

In contrast to our magical experience in Slovenia was the time we traveled to Argentina for an event in Buenos Aires years later. The General again was to present a keynote speech and attend a VIP dinner and we discussed in advance how much we were looking forward to sampling the beef for which Argentina is famous. I also shared that I was hoping his hosts would throw in a tango demonstration if not an actual lesson. He didn't exactly embrace the idea, but after a bit of cajoling on my part, the General agreed he wouldn't rule it out if offered the opportunity.

Once again, we hid our disappointment when served fancy French cuisine instead of the traditional Argentinian delicacies we had been craving. As for entertainment, instead of the tango, we were given a performance of a South American version of Cirque du Soleil. During the performance, one aerial acrobat flew overhead propelled by a jetpack emitting bursts of fiery sparks—so close above my head I felt the sharp tingle of sparks reminiscent of how a child feels when holding a Fourth-of-July sparkler. Luckily, the General was seated far enough away that he did not share in my risk of catching fire.

* * *

When clients would ask me about General Powell's favorite foods, I would assure them and say that given his long career in the military there was no need to plan anything out of the ordinary, as he was used to eating bugs and mud. That was an exaggeration of course, and would have made him roll his eyes had he heard me say it. But my point was to let his hosts know that, unlike storied celebrities with outrageous tastes and demands, the General only wanted a couple of cans of Diet Coke in his suite and he would be fine otherwise. If we needed room service, I reassured them that at most for dinner he would order spaghetti Bolognese (his favorite), a burger or Caesar salad, perhaps with a glass of red wine. In the mornings, he would stick with making coffee in his suite, claiming he didn't need breakfast. (As I knew better, with a laugh I would let the clients know that I would order toast and eggs over easy with bacon for me. I'd then walk half of it down the hall to share with him. He never turned me down.) But that's it. Nothing extraordinary. Again, his preference was always simple comfort food.

On the speaking circuit and in his book, *It Worked For Me*, he expanded in great detail on what he called "hot dog diplomacy." In his hometown of New York City, he claimed there was nothing better than "a dirty water dog," a type of hotdog sold from little pushcarts on the city street corners by hardworking entrepreneurs who were almost always from the immigrant and first-generation families of New York. He rejoiced whenever he could share this specialty with one of his foreign counterparts. He always ordered his with mustard and "that red onion relish you can only get in New York City." On one occasion when he asked me to pick him up at the airport (where I immediately handed over the keys and let him drive), he proudly handed me one of these beloved New York dirty water dogs, which he had cradled in damp wax paper and tinfoil the whole way home on the shuttle, just for me.

* * *

When we traveled by private plane, I always confirmed our catering needs with Roy Oakley, our charter plane provider. For short trips, we were content with the onboard snacks of diet Coke, water, and a little can of Pringles (and maybe a little pack of Oreos). Other times we would simply grab a Subway sandwich from the airport gas station convenience store and eat it on the plane. I often chided the General I'd never allow him to misbehave like some speakers and celebrities we well knew who went nuts with catering demands to rival the cost of the planes themselves. It was a joke of course, but also a sad commentary on the wild excesses demanded by some people who should know better. Happily, I was preaching to the choir, as his needs were always conscientiously simple.

Earlier I made a passing reference to my youthful ballet classes, so it shouldn't be a surprise when I admit I'd always wanted to see the Bolshoi Ballet in Russia. During my years with General Powell, I had two opportunities. During the summer of 1997, Lisa Walker (now Hart), a beloved friend from my first job out of college, and I were going to travel to Moscow to visit Elisa Gambino Broffman, a dear friend since kindergarten, who with her husband was stationed there as producers for CNN.

I'd planned our trip to coincide with the General and Mrs. Powell's vacation in the Mediterranean. During the two weeks I'd be gone, the General was scheduled to fly home in the middle for an event with the American Veterinary Medical Association in Baltimore before rejoining Mrs. Powell for the rest of their vacation. I made all the arrangements and hoped everything would be fine, even though (and especially because) this was the first and only time I'd be on vacation during one of his events.

As part of our visit, Elisa had gotten tickets for us to see a Bolshoi performance and I was thrilled. Unfortunately, for reasons that were never fully explained, on the day of our planned departure the Russian foreign ministry denied my visa (but not Lisa's), so within hours of our confirmed flight, the trip was canceled.

This meant of course that I was home and available to take care of the General when he flew back Washington for his event with the veterinarians. On the day of the event, when the General's trusted driver Page Parvez and I picked him up for the trek to Baltimore, General Powell wanted to stop en route to grab a quick supper since the event didn't include a meal although it was dinner time. With his usual good humor and affinity for ribbing me whenever possible he proclaimed, "Leslie, isn't going through the McDonald's drive-through with Page and me much more fun than seeing some ol' ballet in Moscow?" I could only grouse and let him know that sharing a Big Mac and strawberry milkshake with them clearly did not compare with what I was missing. Of course, the two men laughed while I continued to grumble and dream of what might have been.

Years after our time at the State Department, General Powell was asked by the head of a Russian bank to be a keynote speaker for an international gathering of investment bankers. On the evening before the meeting and speeches, the bank president hosted a VIP reception at the Bolshoi Theatre—yes, *the* Bolshoi Theatre of my dreams—and as part of the evening's agenda, the reception guests were invited to attend a performance of Sergei Prokofiev's "Ivan the Terrible."

Although ballet would not have made the General's top ten list of things he would ever want to do, I choose to believe he accepted the invitation so I could finally see the world-renowned corps de ballet. If anyone ever says otherwise, well, to quote the General with his oft heard saying, "That's my story and I'm sticking to it."

After the first of the two-act performance, the bank president offered to whisk the General away to a private dinner. General Powell accepted the invitation but, without hesitation or even looking at me, asked if he could leave me to enjoy the performance to the end. Sure enough, with one whispered aside, the bank president made the arrangements to allow me to remain in the Tsar's box sipping champagne through the second act. Surely, it was a dream come true, and I basked in the thrill of watching the performers on stage in that magical setting. I also delighted in the reminder of how well the General knew me.

The General and his host left me with my own "babysitter," who was tasked with taking me out to dinner afterwards to fill the time until the General's dinner was over. My handler was an exceptionally gracious young man who worked for the bank and, as we left the theater, he courteously asked where I wished to go for dinner. Having never been to Moscow before, I didn't know what to say other than I'd be grateful to try Muscovian or Russian cuisine, which was known for its world-famous caviar.

He surprised me with his response, saying there wasn't anything in Moscow he would recommend that showcased good Russian cuisine and that he suggested a Middle Eastern restaurant instead. As we both were aide-de-camps, we kept our cell phones close at hand while waiting for the signal alerting us that our respective bosses were on the move. Nevertheless, we enjoyed the meal and, in all honesty, that dinner with its assortment of grilled meats and authentic mezes was probably the tastiest Middle Eastern food I had ever been served.

As for the food enjoyed by the General and the president of the bank? They ended up being served French cuisine. *Bien sûr.*

This is circa 1997 and is likely the first posed picture we took together.

At a Dreamforce event in Tokyo with Marc Benioff, Chair, CEO & co-founder of Salesforce. As usual, I'm in the background.

General Powell is shaking hands with the Foreign Minister, the former Ambassador of Slovenia to the U.S., and I'm checking the staging.

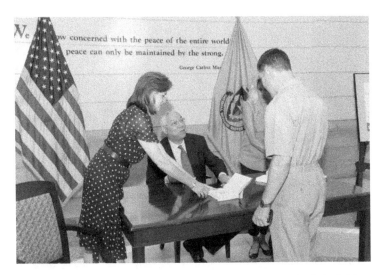

A book signing of the General's book, *It Worked For Me: In Life &*
Leadership, at the National Defense University, Ft. Lesley McNair.

Escorting the President of Mexico and Mrs. Fox into
the Benjamin Franklin Room for Secretary Powell's
first State Luncheon as Secretary of State.

Secretary Powell swearing-in Kenneth Hackett and Christine Todd Whitman to the Millennium Challenge Corporation, July 2004.

A joyful book signing at Ft. Belvoir's PX just in time for the holidays.

Discovering the Secretary of State at my surprise 40th birthday party, the week of 5 February 2003. Laughing with joy in the background on the left are Ambassador Lucky Roosevelt and dear friend Randy Bumgardner, and on the right is Mrs. Powell.

Laughing over memories of seeing Mama Mia together with Donny Osmond.

Down in the Bunker playing with the Star Wars lightsaber George Lucas gave him. Yes, it's real.

Shared joy.

In the Red Sox dugout waiting to throw out
the first pitch. To blend in, I wore red.

General Powell signed a picture to "Grandma Kitty" that hung over my
grandmother's bed for years at Westport Nursing Home in Richmond.

At General Powell's surprise 80th birthday party: Grant Green,
Ken Duberstein, Marybel Batjer, the birthday boy, Peggy
Cifrino, Rich Armitage, and me. I may be the baby of the
bunch but we all worked in the Reagan administration.

Peggy Cifrino and I, the General's two assistants,
pose with General and Mrs. Powell at the unveiling
ceremony of his official Secretary of State portrait.

Briefing Secretary Powell on the official plane en route to Kyiv for the inauguration of the Ukrainian President, January 2005.

In the shadow of my General.

With Lisa Fikes at his annual backyard pool party
for the Colin Powell Leadership Club.

Even in white tie attire,
General Powell was ever
eager to play for laughs.

Having tea with a world champion Sumo Wrestler
at a Sumo Stable in Tokyo, September 1997.

Escorting former Presidents George H. W. Bush and Bill Clinton
after their meeting with Secretary Powell regarding relief efforts
following the tsunami that hit Southeast Asia, December 2004.

Laying a wreath at the Korean Military
Academy in Seoul, Republic of Korea.

Attending "On Golden Pond" at the Kennedy Center
to see General Powell's daughter Linda play the
part of James Earl Jones' daughter on stage.

Although we hated selfies, we took this one in the Bunker in late winter 2021. It is the last picture for which we posed together.

The family picture the General insisted we take at the Richmond
Forum: my brother Win Lautenslager, my mother Margaret
Lautenslager, Aunt Patricia and Uncle Jim Duke, Aunt Anne and
Uncle Moe Robertson (with General Powell and me in the middle).

A meeting with royal government leaders in the United Arab Emirates.

General Powell wanted to rest in peace
"down with the troops." And he is.

9.

All That Glitters

"So help me, the thing looks like a pet's headstone."
—Colin Powell, "It Worked For Me," p. 258

The old saying, "Beauty is in the eye of the beholder," is never truer than in the context of gifts and gift giving. From my vantage point behind the scenes with General Powell, I developed an expertise in the finer points of gift exchanges that are not only critical at high levels of government but can be equally helpful to anyone. As it would be a shame to let what I learned from his many years of experience giving and receiving gifts go to waste, I'll happily share some of our more notable observations.

After holding the nation's most senior positions over decades, General Powell had been given many gifts from foreign leaders on behalf of their governments. Although many of these items by law became the property of the U.S. government, the Powell home was still filled with a wide array of these treasures. On the speaking circuit, leaders of organizations also frequently gave him gifts in appreciation for his participation in their event as well as for his service to the nation.

As beautiful as a priceless engraved crystal bowl is, though, just how many does any one person need? How many walls in a home are available to hang framed plaques commemorating an event? Like most people in the public eye, General Powell constantly had to deal with deciding how to handle one more of anything. Over time, his storage closets were filled with this largesse.

Even those of us who aren't parents likely have had a child give us a crayon-colored masterpiece that reflects that child's creativity and love. The smiling face looking up seeking praise can produce panic in us when we have no idea if the proffered gift was meant to be a fairytale princess, a frog, or a spaceship. Fear of saying the wrong thing often reduces us to utter an all-purpose, "Oh, how wonderful!"

Now, take the fear of disappointing that hopeful child and apply it to the official and diplomatic world. Here, the wrong reaction can have diplomatic repercussions that reflect horribly on both the giver and the recipient.

At the State Department, the most challenging cases could be avoided by having the gift exchange taken care of behind the scenes, "protocol to protocol," rather than between Secretary Powell and the visiting dignitaries. This formal choreography of the exchange allowed both sides to be prepared, proper courtesies to be observed, and the requisite expressions of gratitude to be written and provided after the fact.

This level of formality is rarely found outside of official government situations, however. On the speaking circuit, many gift presentations were part of the event. Often our hosts were excited about a special "surprise" they wanted to present to General Powell at the end of a program. To them, it was very important it be kept a secret, as they had hopes of seeing his unguarded reaction when the gift materialized. Whenever I learned of such a plan, I had the General's blessing to lie. And I lied shamelessly.

As soon as I learned of the planned surprise, I would convince our hosts to let me in on it by *promising* (fingers crossed behind my back) not to tell the General. Following my mantra of "always make the boss look good," I would then tell him as soon as possible. In any situation, the General did not want to be surprised and I certainly never wanted to surprise him. Instead, letting him know as much about the gift as I could was part of my pre-event briefings to "make him smart" about every aspect of the program. When I revealed the secret though, I would emphasize it was tremendously important to feign surprise when it was given to him. No matter the gift, he needed to look not only surprised but delighted.

It is far easier to appear "delighted" if told in advance that the village's resident donkey was just named in your honor. Likewise, it takes some preparation to show appreciation instead of visceral shock when witnessing the ceremonial sacrifice of an animal in the ultimate sign of honor as you disembark the plane.

Imagine you have just been given a sculpture of your likeness carved out of butter or a framed portrait done in birdseed, and the artist is waiting excitedly for your reaction while a large crowd looks on. A heads up beforehand prevents an unguarded reaction and with it a public relations nightmare.

Even so, there were times when no matter how much we knew in advance, reacting properly was challenging. Once, at the end of an event, General Powell was presented with a heavy piece of granite. One side had been polished and across its surface the General's likeness had been engraved with a laser, along with the dates and details of the event. Clearly, a lot of thought and effort (and money) had gone into the gift, but somehow the resemblance to something appropriate for a cemetery had escaped their notice. Once in the car and on his way to the airport out of sight of his hosts, he could not help but exclaim with a laugh, "A pet headstone with my face on it! Really?"

Nevertheless, his thank-you note expressed his appreciation for his hosts' thoughtfulness.

At the beginning of his tenure as Secretary of State, he asked me to explore different ideas for what would be his signature gift to his foreign counterparts. As with all official gifts, the item needed to be made in America and reflect our history in some way. We also wanted something that was distinctly representative of General Powell.

While stationed in Ft. Leavenworth early in his military career, General Powell had initiated the first monument to honor Buffalo Soldiers, members of the 10th Cavalry Regiment of the U.S. Army, formed in 1866. The beautiful monument that resulted from his initiative is a Buffalo Soldier rearing up on horseback, done by a talented sculptor named Eddie Dixon of Lubbock, Texas. I suggested we see if the artist would allow small desk top versions be made to give as gifts.

Sure enough, for the next four years, Secretary Powell's signature gift to senior leaders was a small version of the historic sculpture. Each was signed and placed inside a specially designed box along with a brief history. Reflecting American history and Secretary Powell's background, I doubt anything could have been more appropriate for him to give.

* * *

Early in his career General Powell was well known for repairing and trading old, beat-up Volvos as a form of relaxation. Over the quarter century I worked for him, I lost track of how many stories he told me of different cars he'd tinkered on (including mine) and all those he had been given to fix. I also lost count of how many thoughtful people around the world had wanted to give him their beat-up Volvos, certain there would be no greater gift for him to enjoy.

I once attended a workshop at the National Archives that included a session called "Tokens and Treasures: Gifts of State and What Becomes of Them." John Laster, Director of Congressional Affairs, National Archives and Records Administration, was asked about some of the more unusual gifts he had seen over his career. With a laugh, Mr. Laster said that at the beginning of the Obama administration it became public knowledge that the newly elected President's two young daughters liked hula hoops. Suddenly, vast quantities of hula hoops were sent to the White House (and consequently, the National Archives) from people from around the world.

Likewise, I remember when Lady Diana Spencer became engaged to Prince Charles, it was revealed that salmon was one of her favorite foods. Consequently, everywhere she went her hosts designed menus around salmon in hopes of pleasing her. Unfortunately, after being served every possible preparation of salmon wherever she went, she quickly wearied of eating her formerly favored fish.

These gifts of Volvos, hula hoops, and salmon were gestures of goodwill by people with kind and generous hearts, hoping to please the recipients with something they liked. However, William Shakespeare reminds us in the oft-quoted line from his play *As You Like It*, there can be "too much of a good thing."

* * *

General Powell often received packages from Amazon. He was constantly ordering things online, too, and delighted in how efficient the process was, gleefully crowing about how quickly items appeared on his front stoop. Amongst his ordered deliveries were also gifts from loved ones and thank you gifts from organizations following an event he had attended. Upon receiving one of these, he immediately called me asking, "Leslie, who is this guy? Do we know him? Is he from some recent gig?"

The box held a large gourmet basket laden with all sorts of delicacies and several bottles of fine wine. It was a lovely gift, but General Powell had no idea who the giver was. The note tucked inside held only a "please enjoy" style message followed by a name. It was clearly someone assuming a personal connection and not a company soliciting business, but the name was a common one and unfamiliar. I scoured our files of recent events, checking boards of directors and sponsor lists, but I never found anyone by that name. We even tracked down recent head table guest lists, thinking that maybe the gentleman had been seated with the General at some dinner. No luck.

Amazon.com's data included nothing beyond the sender's name. Contacting Amazon directly wasn't helpful either—the Amazon.com folk can only send a note back to the giver saying, "The recipient doesn't know you." No one wants to acknowledge a basket of fine wine by sending such a harsh declaration back to the generous benefactor.

We never did figure out who our mystery gift giver was despite spending far too much time trying to track him down. It was an example, though, of basic Gift Giving 101 rules we followed carefully.

For tangible gifts:

Unless intentionally giving a gift anonymously, make sure it is well understood from whom (and to whom) it is intended.

Make sure the gift card is included with the gift. I have been known to attack tables of gifts at wedding receptions with scotch tape to affix loose cards to their respective boxes to save the bride and groom from post-wedding headaches writing thank-you notes. I even had scotch tape tucked away in my purse for just that purpose at the General's daughter's wedding.

When gift giving is done in an official capacity, keep detailed records of what has been given over multiple years. No one really needs yet another engraved crystal bowl or framed piece of art (or even a Buffalo Soldier) commemorating the same occasion each year.

For intangible gifts:

When sending a text, "give the gift" of identifying yourself. Too many times, the General and I would laugh while trying to figure out mystery texters sending messages from cellphones with no caller ID.

Even though the General was recognized wherever he went, he would still offer his hand and identify himself. We often met others in mix and mingle events and had trouble remembering names even though we may have met some guests before. I always assume I'm not remembered, so rather than make someone struggle, I follow the General's lead and offer my name from the start.

Regarding name tags: it's always better to wear it on the right side so it's visible when shaking hands. General Powell, of course, drew the line at wearing nametags. To placate eager staffers trying to meet their bosses' requirements that *all* guests wear nametags, I would take the General's and wear it alongside mine. (When other guests noticed me wearing his name badge, it often served as a delightful ice breaker.)

General Powell and I had fun with gifts for each other over the years. Scattered amidst the many sweet and meaningful ones, there were plenty meant in jest. Guessing what was inside wrinkly wrapped packages with "To L2, Love, CP" scribbled across the top in black Sharpie was always a game for me. Some of his funniest gems included potato scrubbing gloves, chia pets, a Snuggie blanket, a Madame Alexander Snow White collectible doll, and an elaborate ratchet set (which I still don't know how to use).

Mine to him on occasion were just as playful. Over the years I gave him a box of hammers (each with a name I'd scribbled in black Sharpie along the handle of someone we knew), a coloring book of caricatures I'd drawn of him, a bag of items from every one-dollar-or-less bin at a local hardware store, and an apron sporting a series of funny pictures of him (poking fun at his announcing to me "Real men don't cook.").

The General preferred to do his own home repairs rather than pay for an expert to come to the house. The year there was a leak in the backyard from an underground pipe, the "little" hole he dug trying to find the errant pipe ended up growing to several feet long before he finally gave up and called in a professional. For his April birthday, during those days of his expanding swamp, the present I gave was not nearly as significant as how I'd wrapped it.

My "wrapping paper" was a couple feet of muddy lawn sod with several yards of twine used as a ribbon, wrapped around it and tied into a bow. He had to admit my wrapping that year was a masterpiece and apropos.

Often when General Powell gave a keynote speech at a college or university, my contacts would ask me for gift ideas. I always reassured them a gift was not necessary and explained teasingly that since he already had at least twelve of everything he really didn't need to add to the collection. Even so, as gift giving was so often part of the established choreography of the event, they would frequently insist that *something* be given. My suggestion then would usually be something symbolic—say, plant a tree on campus, direct resources within the university to honor students in his name, etc. I was delighted when my contact at one school came up with the perfect gift—so perfect that I broke my own rule and when time came for my "make him smart" briefing, explained to the General that this time I wouldn't let him know it in advance. The gift was far too thoughtful, and just this once I really wanted him to be able to enjoy it as a surprise. I may have had to reassure him many times on that score, but in the end he trusted me.

At the conclusion of his speech, the guests took their seats following a well-deserved standing ovation. The university president then called two members of the senior class to join him and General Powell on stage. The young woman and young man introduced themselves and proceeded to explain that they were happy to say they had no gift to give General Powell. There would be no gift to unwrap, no gift to take home, no gift to hang or display. Instead, they were joyfully giving him their pledge on behalf of not only the senior class but the students throughout their college community that they would do better—they would strive to follow his example and would be better citizens of the world, more optimistic, fairer, and kinder. They pledged to live their lives from that day forward in ways that would make him proud.

Even though I knew what to expect, my tears—like those on the faces of many in the audience—flowed readily in hearing their pledge, the precious gift of their future years.

The tears on the General's smiling face showed how much their generosity meant to him.

In thinking back to that wonderful moment, I cannot help but think of the General's eleventh rule: "*Have a vision. Be demanding.*"

These young people had a vision of how they wanted to live their lives, and chose a very demanding yet rewarding one when they chose to follow the General as their role model.

Before we went to the State Department, General Powell often told me, "You gotta meet my Lisa" before waxing poetic about his friend Lisa Fikes (*née* Navarra), the Associate for Youth and Children's Ministries at his church in McLean, St. John's Episcopal. Apparently, he was doing the same thing with Lisa by telling her, "You gotta meet my Leslie" before describing me in equally glowing ways. Since the General had two beloved nieces named Lisa and Leslie, there was a bit of symmetry to his trying to get us to meet. Even so, much like the exasperation one gets fending off well-intentioned friends who try to set up blind dates, I could not help thinking (though never saying out loud), "I can make my own friends, sir. I don't really need your help, thank you very much."

I—we—were able to keep his friend matchmaking efforts at bay for many months until a Christmas party at his house in 2000, just weeks before he was sworn in as Secretary of State. I was with Mrs. Powell and my friend Randy Bumgardner in the dining room and had just picked up one of the Powells' miniature Yorkshire terriers (adorned with a red plaid taffeta ruffle), when I heard the General bellow my name from the front door. Even though I did not literally jump to attention as one in uniform would, as always I came when he called. As soon as I turned the corner and was in his sight, he gestured to the open door and proclaimed with a big self-satisfied smile on his face, "Leslie, Lisa. Lisa, Leslie!"

I am sure that was not the first, last, or only time the General took delight in reminding me that sometimes he knew me better than I knew myself. From that moment, Lisa and I have been the dearest of friends and continue to be grateful for that loving gift of friendship our beloved General gave us both.

The General's three children, his daughter-in-law, his son-in-law, and I all went to the College of William & Mary. A favorite holiday tradition we all enjoyed on campus as undergraduates was gathering in the historic Wren Building Courtyard just before fall semester's final exams to hear the president of the university's annual reading of *"How the Grinch Stole Christmas"* by children's book author, Dr. Seuss.

Truly, the General's best gifts reflected the wisdom of Dr. Seuss as observed by the Grinch: *"It came without ribbons; it came without tags. It came without packages, boxes, or bags."*

10.

With Stars of Stage
and Screen

"A dream doesn't become reality through magic; it takes sweat, determination, and hard work."
 —Colin Powell

I remember the moment I realized General Powell was more than a revered military leader. When the 50th Annual Tony Awards aired on June 2, 1996, I had only been working with him for a few weeks and was home watching the show when I was stunned to see the General in one of the musical numbers. He was not performing in person on stage of course, but his face on the cover of his autobiography, *My American Journey*, was. The renowned tap dancer and choreographer, Savion Glover, star of *Bring in 'da Noise, Bring in 'da Funk*, was performing a piece from the show with the General's autobiography clutched under his arm. As the Broadway show depicts black history from slavery to modern day through tap, this amazing dancer used the book as a prop to help tell the story.

In that moment, I realized my General was more than a Washington name. I called him that night and told him that being on the Tonys meant he really must be famous. He laughed, and again welcomed me to his world.

General Powell enjoyed the arts and had a great affinity for music and theater. His appreciation for people who had mastered their craft included those in the creative arts, examples that it takes hard work to make dreams come true.

It was a wonderful adventure to be part of his world as he crossed paths with stars of stage and screen.

One of my favorite recurring events while General Powell was Secretary of State was the annual Kennedy Center Honors Dinner. The Kennedy Center Honors performance is usually televised a couple days after Christmas, but the awards are actually presented by the Secretary of State the first week of December at a black-tie dinner with the Diplomatic Reception Rooms providing the perfect setting to celebrate the talents of our best performing artists.

Assisting at these events while dressed in a long gown was always a highlight of my holiday season as I shepherded world-renowned stars and their guests. It was great fun to witness famous celebrities acting like their own fans whenever they were awed meeting someone for the first time. Even celebrities have heroes.

I have many fond memories of these events. When Annette Benning asked me to find and tell her husband she was going to powder her nose, I discovered that Warren Beatty, like many husbands, is much happier at social events with his wife nearby. He thanked me profusely (again and again and again), admitting he was a bit lost without her. Sir Elton John was incredibly gracious with impeccable manners, and his partner, David Furnish (now his husband), asked me to identify guests he did not yet know. Loretta Lynn, dressed in a maraschino red dress with multiple flounces, eagerly accepted my help with a wardrobe malfunction.

I'll admit I had my favorites among the guests. I always looked forward to seeing the charming and lovely Christine Baranski, as well as Courtney B. Vance and his wife, Angela Bassett, who both have that wonderful talent for making anyone near them feel like the most important person in the room.

Secretary Powell's remarks during the award presentations were always inspiring. He recognized the talents and accomplishments of each honoree, lacing well-researched and heartfelt remarks with humor. He loved being "shameless," and when delivering his tribute to Chita Rivera, belted out a few lines from "I Want to Be in America" from *West Side Story*. When she tried to respond in kind, he threatened to out-sing her in a musical duel and the guests roared with laughter. During his tribute to Sir Elton John, Secretary Powell showed his serious side, exploring the song *Little Nikita* and how it reminded him of his time in uniform during the Cold War.

Whenever General Powell traveled or attended dinner parties with which I was not involved, I would still monitor my phone closely. It was never a question of if he would call, only when. For events with musical entertainment, he would check in to let me hear the music in the background—sometimes with him singing along. I once got a call with him singing an old Rod Stewart song—with Rod Stewart singing beside him. Anytime he shared the music, I could sense the joy in his voice as he shouted through the surrounding din. Afterwards, it was not unusual to see pictures of him dancing on stage with various celebrities, such as Jamie Foxx. I am sure I was not the only person General Powell called to share his delight with during these musical performances. Like a kid in a candy store, he simply could not resist sharing the moment.

The General knew how much I admire Dame Julie Andrews

and want to be like her ("when I grow up," I'd say). Her embodiment of Rodgers and Hammerstein's *Cinderella* put stars in my eyes as a child. I still yearn to be "practically perfect in every way" like Mary Poppins, and I would certainly like to mirror her Maria von Trapp in many ways.

Once during a summer vacation, General and Mrs. Powell had the pleasure of dining with Dame Julie at a small dinner party given by some of their dearest friends. Although the three had met previously when as Secretary of State he had presented the Kennedy Center Honor to her, this was a magical night. He sent me updates throughout the evening and forwarded a picture they took together. He confirmed the hills were indeed alive with the sound of music (though I question how many hills are on Long Island beaches), the chef served Wiener schnitzel, and the local floral designer provided a beautiful centerpiece of Edelweiss. He gleefully described to me the evening's smallest details, which I savored, but the joy he shared meant even more.

As he was enjoying his enchanted evening, I was at home watching television and coincidentally stumbled across the 2001 Disney movie, "The Princess Diaries," in which Dame Julie plays Queen Clarisse Renaldi of the fictional Kingdom of Genovia. Towards the end of this film, the Queen says to her executive assistant, "Did you hear that?" and the assistant responds, "Not if you didn't want me to." And I laughed out loud. Knowing General Powell was dining with *the* Julie Andrews while I was hearing on screen an exchange he and I often had almost word for word was comical. As my function was to remain in the background, I was privy to all sorts of confidential discussions. What a joy to have his confidence.

* * *

The General loved music and on days I joined him in his home office, the Bunker, I never knew what to expect as I descended the stairs into the basement. Would he be listening to Broadway show-tunes, or gospel choirs on a televangelist's morning program? From his parents' Jamaican heritage, he grew up listening to Calypso and was delighted to meet The Mighty Sparrow, his favorite Calypso singer, at an event we attended in Trinidad and Tobago. He and opera tenor Placido Domingo sang happy birthday to each other over the phone every year from wherever they were in the world at the time. He adored the Welsh singer Dame Shirley Bassey, and was a fount of random knowledge about Maurice Gibb's brief marriage to Lulu, Rod Stewart's ukulele playing background singer, and the behind-the-scenes soap opera-like stories of Fleetwood Mac. But of all the pop musicians in the world, none held a candle to his beloved ABBA.

When he was Secretary of State, he was in New York for the Opening of the United Nations General Assembly, and the musical *Mamma Mia* was playing on Broadway. Before the days of intensive bilateral and multilateral meetings with President Bush and other world leaders, we scheduled an evening of precious free time to see it. I purchased orchestra seat tickets for Secretary and Mrs. Powell, four members of his senior staff, and myself. With the Diplomatic Security team coordinating the security arrangements, I worked with the theater management to ensure all was in place for our attendance.

The Secretary's arrival at the theater was uneventful and we quietly took our seats without notice. As I sat down across the aisle and one row in front of the Secretary, he motioned me over.

His serious face was soon wreathed in a smile as he whispered, "Take a look at who's sitting on the other side of Alma."

I did as he directed and recognized former teen idol Donny Osmond laughing delightedly with Mrs. Powell. The two of them seemed to be having a wonderful time getting acquainted.

Not to be outdone, I told the Secretary to watch me walk down the aisle a few rows and look at the person seated beside me when I turned around.

It was Israeli Prime Minister Benjamin Netanyahu.

Then it was show time and I scurried back to my seat. The performance that followed was as wonderful as we had hoped. I had arranged with the theater manager to take Secretary Powell and our merry little State Department team backstage to meet the cast as soon as the curtain call was over.

What fun! As soon as we arrived, the cast surrounded the Secretary and laughingly explained that though they hadn't been told he was in the audience, they had easily recognized him long before intermission. Of the audience members visible from the stage, he was the most animated, singing each song word for word. As for the standing ovation at the curtain call, it was impossible to miss him dancing and singing along enthusiastically.

A good time was truly had by all—a teen heart throb, a leader of the Middle East, *Mamma Mia*'s cast and crew, as well as the rest of the audience. But no one that night enjoyed it more than the Secretary of State of the United States of America.

Over the course of several appearances together at the National Memorial Day concert, General Powell became friends with Alfie Boe, the English tenor best known for his portrayal of Jean Valjean in *Les Misérables* in the West End of London and later on Broadway. They kept in touch by email and when Alfie was asked to reprise his role in a *Les Mis* revival on Broadway, he invited General and Mrs. Powell to come up to New York City for a performance. Ever thoughtful (with our shameless prodding), the General replied his two assistants (Peggy Cifrino and I) were devoted *Les Mis* fans and were begging to be included as well. Sure enough, the four of us took a train up to NYC for a Wednesday matinee as special guests of Monsieur 2-4-6-0-1 himself. (For those who are not *Les Mis* devotees, 2-4-6-0-1 is Jean Valjean's prison number and factors into the plot and lyrics.)

The show was breathtaking. With the four of us seated side-by-side, it was never apparent whose silent sobs caused the seats to shake at any given time. No matter how many times I've seen the show, my tears flow freely, so I always arrive well equipped with tissues and readily pass packets down the row as needed.

Alfie told the General in advance he wanted us to wait a bit before catching our return train, so that we could join him on stage. As soon as the theater emptied, we were escorted up onto the stage and had a delightful time meeting the cast. When the General introduced me to Mister Boe, I was amazed at how sensitive he seemed as he gently put his hand on my shoulder, looked into my eyes with deep concern, and asked, "This is a really meaningful story for you, isn't it?" I was spellbound, marveling that he could read me like an open book.

That fantasy was dashed the minute I looked in the ladies' room mirror before leaving the theater. Staring back at me from the glass was the image of a crying clown from an old black velvet painting. Mr. 2-4-6-0-1 had not seen into my soul at all, but had simply observed the vivid black stripes of mascara trailing down my cheeks.

And the General had not shared a single word of warning! He'd just grinned.

*   *   *

For an event in Beijing, General Powell was the keynote speaker for an international investment bank. Following a full day of meetings and speeches, we attended a gala dinner for several hundred people outdoors in the Forbidden City. During our preparations, we'd been assured the temperature on March 9th was always around 69 degrees Fahrenheit and we had packed accordingly. Unfortunately, an inch of snow fell on the city that day and by nightfall temperatures had plummeted well below freezing. Nevertheless, the dinner was held outdoors as planned. Although there were light tarp-like canopies to prevent snow from falling into our plates, it was tremendously cold. We were seated at the VIP table in the middle of the gathering, but the tall heating lamps stood in the outer corners, far away from us. Holding the metal chopsticks from our place settings was painful, as there was a real danger of our skin freezing onto the metal.

Ever the military leader who was mindful of his troops' welfare, General Powell almost seethed when he saw that the young girls serving us were only dressed in thin traditional silk cheongsams. No matter how beautifully attired they were or how diligently they took care of us, the General was fuming and said through clenched teeth that if he'd been in charge he'd have demoted whomever had placed these young girls in danger of hypothermia.

Despite the punishing cold, the dinner went on with an elaborate performance on a huge stage. After Chinese acrobats and the Peking Opera performed, the headliner came out and was none other than Lionel Richie. As he took the stage and looked out at the shivering audience, he gave the General a subtle salute, probably unnoticed by anyone else, before announcing (as he wrapped a long woolen scarf around his neck) there would be no ballads nor love songs that evening. Instead, "All Night Long" we would be "Dancing on the Ceiling" for warmth. What a gift. For the rest of the performance, under the guise of dancing, we gratefully jumped up and down trying to keep warm.

In 2008, General Powell was invited to give a keynote address in London for an event called "Africa Rising." He had been asked by Nigerian businessman Nduka Obaigbena, founding Chairman and Editor-in-Chief of THISDAY Media Group and a Duke of the Owa Kingdom, to give brief remarks adding a bit of gravitas to an otherwise celebratory event showcasing African fashion, music, and diamond jewelry artistry. World renowned super models Alek Wek and Tyson Beckford graced the runway between musical segments provided by international singing sensations Seal and Christina Aguilera, along with several talented African musicians.

Even though the General's official role was limited to opening the event with ten-minutes of serious remarks, his words left the standing-room only crowd at Prince Albert's Hall inspired. Our hosts told us we could leave as soon as he finished his remarks, but by then General Powell was well into the spirit of the evening and decided to stay.

The rest of the evening was terrific. The models wore spectacular diamond jewelry and were attired beautifully in clothes designed by both up-and-coming and well-established African fashion designers. We were in prime seats next to the catwalk running down the middle of the orchestra section and could almost reach out and touch the models.

Towards the end of the program, a Nigerian hip-hop group called Olu Maintain took the stage and soon the audience was moving to their beat. After a couple songs, they asked to have the house lights turned up, saying that they couldn't let the evening go by without inviting "a very special guest to join us on stage—but where is he? Where is he?"

I knew what was coming next. As the lights came up, search lights scanned the crowd, and while the lead singer continued speaking, I reached down with what I meant to be a death grip and grabbed the back of General Powell's calf. Through clenched teeth I growled, "Do *not* embarrass Mrs. Powell. Do *not* embarrass your kids. Do *not* embarrass your grandchildren. And. Do. *Not*. Embarrass. Me!"

My pleading was a lost cause, of course. The General's eyes were twinkling and although he hadn't done anything to attract attention, the people around us started chanting and pointing. As soon as he was discovered, he didn't resist being escorted onto the stage to join the group for their next song. The musicians taught him the lyrics (in a language we did not know) and taught him the hip-hop steps. The audience loved it, and he had a ball, my embarrassment doubtless adding to his enjoyment.

It wasn't until later we learned that his hip-hop singing debut was to a popular Nigerian song that satirically extolled the virtues of Nigerian phone scammers. And a recording of his performance can be found on YouTube.

So much for my death grip.

* * *

Few could work a room like General Powell. He knew it was important to his hosts that each guest at a reception be given the chance to shake his hand and share a word. To get through the crowd yet greet everyone, it was essential to avoid "beehives," our term for the surging crowds that would gather around him and follow in his wake. I could part the crowds by body blocking when necessary, but usually he could simply move a few steps to break through to the next cluster. As he circulated, I would remain close enough that our private codes could signal how and when it was time to disappear.

In 1999, we were at the Congressional Award Foundation Gala at the Ronald Reagan Building where General Powell was presenting one of the awards. He worked the VIP reception quicker than expected and before we were caught in a beehive, we escaped to his private hold room across the hall. After a few minutes, we learned that Tom Selleck had arrived and was in the VIP reception we'd just left. Alone. General Powell and I knew the actor would now be in the beehive we had so recently evaded, so I was deputized to rescue him from the chaos.

The General knew I was a long-time fan so my mission was by no means a hardship.

I waded through the crowd and formally announced, "Mr. Selleck, I work with General Powell, and he invites you to join him in his Green Room if you would like." With a look of relief, he eagerly followed me out of the crowd to join the General. As they were old buddies, they had a good catch up and more than a few laughs.

Eventually the other head table guests joined us. One was a woman who greeted the General with an exuberant hug and a kiss, exclaiming she owed him her life. She dramatically described for the gathered guests how years ago, while at a White House dinner, she'd started choking on a piece of chicken and General Powell had rescued her with the Heimlich maneuver. Amidst the laughter after her animated narration of the General's heroic act, Tom Selleck confessed with a laugh that he lived in fear of witnessing someone choking because he had no idea what to do.

Armies are either fighting or training to fight, and so *any* opportunity to perform on-the-spot instruction was too good for General Powell to let pass. Add to that, he never missed a chance to make me blush. Consequently, as soon as the actor shared his fear, what followed was inevitable:

"Tom, worry no more! I'll teach you the Heimlich maneuver here and now!"

And then with twinkling eyes…

"*LESLIE!*"

Immediately, General Powell positioned me, wrapped the handsome actor's arms around my waist just so, and demonstrated to this appreciative and distinguished black-tie attired crowd the appropriate procedures for how to save a life.

From General Powell's famous Thirteen Rules, his "*It can be done!*" certainly applied to this important demonstration.

My only regret? We had no photographer present to capture my once-in-a-lifetime blushingly awkward dance with Magnum P.I.

*   *   *

General Powell was always a voracious reader. In addition to the five newspapers he read every morning, he devoured biographies, memoirs, and books on current affairs. He even read at least one *Harry Potter* book. (The only one I have ever read is the one he gave me after he finished it.) Despite the breadth of his reading tastes, however, I am absolutely certain he never read a romance novel.

Whenever we flew commercially, General Powell preferred the window seat with me on the aisle blocking him from easy recognition by fellow passengers. One morning, after we'd settled in for a flight to the west coast, I looked up into the brilliant blue eyes of a towering six-foot-three-inch man with flowing blonde tresses. As he took his seat in the row behind me across the aisle, I realized it was Fabio, one of the most world-famous romance novel cover models of the 1990s and spokesperson for *I Can't Believe It's Not Butter!*

With the General's "infantry ears" (i.e., some hearing loss from years in the infantry), I knew I'd never be able to explain who Fabio was loudly enough for him to hear without others in our section listening in, so I typed some basic Fabio information for him to read on my phone screen. I even Googled up some romance novel cover art displaying Fabio in all his windblown glory to prepare the General in case they met during the flight.

After our arrival at LAX, as we hurried off the plane to meet our assigned security agent, a heavily accented voice could be heard behind us calling out, "Colin Powell! Colin Powell!" Sure enough, there was Fabio trying to break through the crowd to catch up with us. Judging from the expressions of some of the women nearby, he seemed to be running in slow motion from the pages of a romance novel, his long flowing locks flying behind him.

Getting the General through airports without drawing attention was never easy. This time it was impossible, as two very recognizable men—from two very different worlds—were embracing each other like old friends in a very busy LAX terminal. With an open-mouthed crowd looking on, they chatted a bit before Fabio begged for a picture. The General happily obliged, but then with a twinkle in his eye grabbed my phone and asked Fabio if he would pose with me. Whether by accident or design, the General spent an inordinately long time taking the picture while Fabio held me tightly to his side. This little photo op had me blushing, the General laughing, and the crowd around us growing with many a romance novel lover within it swooning (and probably envying and hating me in equal measure).

We then continued to our respective cars, companionably chatting the whole way. When he said goodbye, Fabio hugged the General and gallantly kissed me on both cheeks before kissing my hand.

From the backseat of our car, the General could only look at me and laugh. And laugh. And laugh.

* * *

Traveling without being recognized was a challenge. Late one night after finishing an event in New York City, we were en route to the airport when we stopped at a drug store so the General could purchase a Valentine card for Mrs. Powell. Once he found what he wanted, I took it up front to purchase it while he escaped to the waiting car. Although we did our best to act covertly, as soon as I got to the check-out counter a knot of other customers gathered and asked breathlessly, "Wait, wait, wait… Was that… was that Denzel?"

When it comes to being shameless, I learned from the best.

I nodded yes.

In early 2005, when General Powell returned to private life, his friend, Prince Bandar, the ambassador of Saudi Arabia and Dean of the Diplomatic Corps, and the prince's wife, Princess Haifa, gave an exquisite and intimate dinner in the General's honor at their home in McLean. It was a lovely affair for just a few dozen of the Powells' closest friends and family. Every moment of the evening was thoughtfully planned—the menu, setting, and hospitality were all exceptional. At the end of the dinner and after a few gracious remarks, Prince Bandar invited the guests to retire to the library for what he described as a little light after-dinner entertainment. Expecting a piano player or perhaps a quartet of musicians, imagine our surprise when we were greeted by the unmistakable voice of Roberta Flack, with full accompaniment.

By the end of this little "light entertainment," we were dancing in the front of the room as if we were in college again. It was an unforgettable and magical evening.

* * *

General Powell's work ethic was remarkable. He valued hard work—demanding it of himself and those under his leadership. He also was a great proponent for knowing that a life well lived should never be just about work. He had an insatiable curiosity about innumerable things outside of the military and global affairs, including a great appreciation for the arts. The example he set was a gift to all those around him. He once said, "Never become so consumed by your career that nothing is left that belongs only to you and your family. Don't allow your profession to become the whole of your existence."

11.

They Should Know Better

"I have run into too many people in public life who think
they turn on the sun every morning."
  —Colin Powell, "It Worked For Me," p. 189

General Powell usually brought out the best in people. However, there were still some occasions we experienced when a few foolish folks misbehaved egregiously. Although I will not reveal the names of the guilty, I will share the situations where their inappropriate behavior may prompt a laugh or provide a lesson in what not to do.

* * *

We have all attended events where a guest or host misbehaved, or we've heard about celebrities making outrageous demands everywhere they go: requiring only red M&Ms, charging designer clothes to the client's hotel bill, being verbally abusive to assistants, or demanding expensive champagne be provided upon arrival anywhere. General Powell and I had a running joke in which he'd pretend to take on the atrocious habits of some people we knew on the speaking circuit, just to rile me up. I always mock-scolded him that only over my dead body would I allow him to act like [Names Redacted], celebrities or dignitaries known for appalling behavior.

I've described some of the fun we had at the Kennedy Center Honors Dinners with the royalty of Hollywood and Broadway. Few invited guests regretted the opportunity to witness artists being honored for their contributions to American culture through the performing arts. Although bad manners are never appropriate, when someone misbehaves at a black-tie gala like these dinners, such behavior is especially objectionable.

The evenings started with a cocktail reception including a formal receiving line with the Secretary of State and Mrs. Powell beside the five guests of honor. To allow for the dinner and time for each honoree to be appropriately recognized, the event had to follow a strict timeline, requiring the receiving line to start shortly after all the honorees arrived.

At one of these dinners however, our timeline was thrown out of balance when the receiving line was delayed by an honoree's absence. While I called the missing guest's assistant multiple times for status reports, Secretary Powell and the other honorees finally formed the line without her, as we could not hold up the entire night's festivities any longer.

Receiving increasingly vague responses each time I spoke with the assistant, I was incensed when the assistant finally admitted the guest was intentionally delaying her appearance, as she wanted to "make an entrance." That is, she wanted to arrive after everyone else was seated so that she could be announced into the room, "allowing" (her word, not mine) everyone to stand as she entered. She clearly wanted to create a sense that the attendees as well as the other four guests of honor were giving her special recognition with their applause and welcome.

As soon as I heard this, I marched right up to the Secretary to whisper the news, and we agreed to proceed with the program as planned in deference to *all* honorees and guests. Furthermore, we decidedly would *not* provide her the opportunity to make an entrance.

We finished the cocktail reception and receiving line and successfully shepherded the guests to their seats. It was well after the first course had been served that the errant guest finally arrived and, no, I did not announce her into the room. We politely seated her as is appropriate for any guest coming late to an event—as quietly and as gracefully as possible

Although I studiously avoided her glares, I knew she was not happy.

Despite her misbehavior, most of the attendees were so caught up in the magic of the evening this prima donna's actions went unnoticed. Imagine how she would have been remembered if we had delayed the evening's activities to appease her whims. Never let the thoughtlessness of one person ruin the experience for others. Whenever possible, defang the diva.

* * *

While on a visit to Kuala Lumpur for an international speaking engagement, I was included at a private luncheon following the big gala event of the night before. Although I was usually seated at large events, it is less common at small intimate ones. On this occasion, however, I was one of the ten guests at a luncheon for the guest of honor, General Powell.

The event was informal with no planned program. The intent was simply to enjoy some lively conversation with an interesting and influential group of people. Guests included the former prime ministers of Malaysia and Australia, and the head of the soon-to-be launched Al Jazeera America.

This was the one (and only) time in my life I seriously considered causing an international incident intentionally. It was a very near thing.

Upon arrival, everyone "made their manners" (a phrase General Powell used for making proper introductions) and enjoyed refreshments and small talk for a few minutes. When it was time for lunch, we were escorted to our seats around a beautifully set table and then seated. During our delicious Malaysian multicourse lunch, one of the guests, known for his temper and extreme views on just about everything, began arguing heatedly about an issue. He dominated the conversation, using crude language not appropriate for polite company as he raged non-stop about his grievances, leaving the other guests aghast at his diatribe during what was supposed to be an enjoyable luncheon. The host was seated directly opposite me and looked like a deer caught in the headlights, frozen in place. Meanwhile, the irate guest, who sat to my left, was so overwrought he repeatedly slammed his fist on the table between us, causing the fine crystal and china to clatter on the table, dangerously close to shattering.

I racked my brain for anything I could do to end his tirade. Finally, in desperation I was reaching for my water glass with plans to "accidentally" knock it over and draw attention away from the misbehaving guest when I caught General Powell's eye. With a grin and a slight shake of his head, like a baseball catcher signaling to the pitcher, the General gave me a subtle (and understood only by me) message: "*Stand down, Mamma Lion. Sheath your claws. I've got this.*"

Sure enough, the General smoothly took command of the conversation and with well-placed humor redirected it, which no other guest had seemed capable of doing. Ever in command, ever the diplomat, the General turned the tenor of the luncheon around, and the fiery orator seated to my left was saved from having ice water spilled in his lap, though it surely would have cooled his rhetoric.

* * *

General Powell was often a keynote speaker at annual meetings for large national associations. He enjoyed preparing for these events by learning as much as he could about the organization's mission and attendees. Learning about challenges the group faced as an industry helped him focus his remarks.

In preparing for his keynote address for the American Library Association (ALA) Annual Conference, we learned a serious challenge the ALA leadership was facing concerned computer access in public libraries. It was a serious matter that involved various issues, such as freedom of speech and the press, as well as the safety of minors with unsupervised computer access. Unfortunately, a syndicated talk-radio personality used the issue for debate on her call-in show. She encouraged her listeners to join her side of the issue, demanding the General cancel his participation in the conference. For weeks on the air, over many broadcasts, she even provided an address where they could send him letters of protest, which they did, also for weeks.

When the show producers called the General's personal office for confirmation that he had been overwhelmed with angry letters, they were told only a handful had been received. In response, on the next show, the radio personality angrily accused the General's office staff of lying, saying she was certain several hundred letters must have been written and sent by her loyal listeners.

No one lied. General Powell received fewer than ten letters. What the radio personality and her producers didn't realize was that the address they'd provided to their audience was incorrect. It had been incorrectly listed in Boy Scout magazines and was supposed to be an address from which Scouts could request Eagle Scout letters from the General. That address had never been his. It had, in fact, been used by the Washington Speakers Bureau once, but at the time of the incident, it belonged to a maxillofacial surgical office.

And so the riled-up radio voice and her loyal listeners continued to vent their ire on the call-in show, never realizing the poor medical specialists were the actual recipients of their letters. The vitriol the radio show produced was unconscionable, with horrible things said about the General, librarians, and their professional association—due in large part to poor research done by the radio show's producers and its star.

Weeks later, the local post office forwarded over a thousand misaddressed letters to me at the actual Washington Speakers Bureau office. As part of his due diligence to prepare for the ALA event, the General wanted to know everything he could about the issue at stake—including the letters' contents. Since my mother was retired and had the time, he asked her to read them all and provide a general sense of their content. The radio personality would have been surprised to learn many of the letter writers' views did not align with hers at all.

The General fulfilled his obligation to the ALA and delivered a terrific keynote speech celebrating professional librarians and acknowledging the challenges they faced. He did not ignore or downplay the pre-event radio battle, but it was not lost on anyone at the event that as a professional soldier he had spent years in uniform defending our freedoms, including that of the First Amendment. If only the radio listeners could have heard him speak.

Although I desperately wanted to contact the radio show host and let her know how inappropriate and ugly her pillorying of the American Librarians Association and General Powell had been, and how her staff had failed miserably by sharing a wrong address, the General reminded me there was nothing to be gained by engaging a bully.

By ignoring this bully, General Powell publicly demonstrated once again the wisdom of one of his many rules of leadership: *"Never take counsel of your fears or naysayers."* He assessed the issue on its merits and used his principles to guide him. As he always did.

* * *

Guests often take elegantly handwritten calligraphy place cards and menus home after events as souvenirs. These are expected and accepted "takeaways." (I even trained the General to save his from events at the White House, Buckingham Palace, and the like to give me later.) Sometimes, though, a guest would stash an extra cookie or piece of bread in a pocket to enjoy later, too, no matter how formal the occasion might be.

There was a particular member of the press corps notorious for scavenging at State Department receptions. She was not always subtle, as we often observed her filling her purse with handfuls of food from the buffet table. Despite this journalist's bad behavior she wrote great articles after events, and she had champions who begged Secretary Powell to keep her on guest lists for this reason.

We learned to grit our teeth behind a smile when she attended a function, and simply hope none of the other guests would notice or be offended. Once however, towards the end of a large official reception in the beautiful Benjamin Franklin Room, two members of my staff frantically relayed to me that they had just seen her tucking silverware into her purse and they weren't sure what to do.

It's one thing to pilfer dinner rolls and cookies—but silver spoons and forks? Not a chance. That's where I drew the line.

I saw where she hovered at the buffet table and hurried towards her. I suspect my raised eyebrow made me look formidable, as the crowd seemed to part before me to allow a direct path toward the larcenous journalist. Before I could reach her though, she looked up and seeing the look in my eye, quickly scuttled away with whatever was in her hand, fleeing both the scene of the crime and my righteous indignation.

Either she improved her technique, or she realized the error of her ways. She was never caught taking anything again.

*   *   *

Along with the mail of that radio letter-writing campaign, General Powell regularly received lots of mail. Much of it was business related, but a fair amount was fan mail. Many people wrote asking for autographs, and others expressed their desire for him to endorse things or make appearances. Keeping up with it was a daily challenge.

One day I was surprised to find a letter with a 20-dollar bill enclosed. Although the letter began in a rather business-like manner, the writer's tenor changed dramatically as he described what he wanted the General to do with that 20-dollar bill, because of some grievance the writer had. Occasionally, an odd piece of mail would arrive from some disgruntled person or someone battling a mental health issue, and these we simply put aside. Because this one came with cash in it, though, I was concerned and let General Powell know its contents. He took the ugly note in stride and told me to donate the cash to a worthwhile cause or simply send it back.

I chose to return it, as I did not want to give the sender license to say General Powell accepted his money. Along with the 20-dollar bill, I included the original letter and a very formal letter from me. Each word was carefully chosen to be as neutral as possible and to allow no room for misunderstanding.

Thank goodness I did that. Years later, my brother, who for many years worked in security, routinely did a search of my name on the internet. Along with various protocol-related entries, he discovered this disgruntled soul had put his letter to General Powell along with my letter of response on the internet. Had I responded in anger or in anything but a neutral manner, I cringe to know it would have been shared freely and indefinitely with the world.

General Powell's famous Thirteen Rules include, "Get mad, then get over it." As difficult as it is to deal with people who misbehave, we would all benefit from this advice.

12.

Playing For Laughs

"Surround yourself with people who take their work seriously, but not themselves, those who work hard and play hard."
—Colin Powell

Every experienced protocol professional is accustomed to leading their principals from point A to B. The key is to lead while staying out of the way keeping their path clear. Opening doors, navigating crowds, and providing silent cues, became second nature with experience.

Snaking through crowded ballrooms to the head table, or rushing to waiting cars, put me in front but with an eye on the General to make sure he followed. At elevators, I held the door and let him in first. It was a choreography we'd perfected and it worked for us so smoothly it went mostly undetected by others.

My leading with his following was a given when "working" an event. However, when he was no longer "on stage" or being official, he was a perfect gentleman. This was probably a combination of his military training and his mother's rearing, and I learned to not insist on playing the lead when "off duty."

Over time, this choreography came naturally to us, but he

had an ever-present twinkle in his eye and was always eager for a chuckle at my expense, which kept me on my toes.

* * *

We had just finished a luncheon event in Cancun, Mexico. The program had gone well, the attendees had been appreciative and the General's closing keynote speech was well received. Our hosts were thrilled their event had ended on a high note, and we were extremely satisfied as we exited the ballroom. Though it was a bit of a crowd, all was well as I shepherded the General to the elevator. Just as we reached the elevator doors, we switched roles as usual, and he held the elevator door for me and some other guests.

As I turned around to face the doors, everyone else in the elevator began laughing, for while I was stepping into the elevator with the other guests and my back was turned to him, General Powell had placed a finger to his lips, nodded his head in my direction, and scurried away. Fortunately, his co-conspirators—i.e., everyone else in the elevator—allowed me to stop the closing doors and wiggle out. I had to break out into a jog to keep him in sight, much to the elevator crowd's delight as well as that of everyone between the General and me. Always a performer, he finally stopped and proclaimed to anyone in earshot, "*She* never *lets me escape!*"

He was often quoted as saying, "You don't know what you can get away with until you try."

* * *

In vaudeville, a stock character in comic routines was called the straight man, and I relished playing that role for the General. It was never planned, but was it ever fun when General Powell lobbed a verbal softball for laughs in my direction. Sometimes he played it simply to give me the opportunity to feign an exasperated school-marm expression as if I were looking at a recalcitrant schoolboy. Other times he was setting me up to provide a witty response.

As I think back, the operative word is "play." General Powell made play out of work on the speaking circuit at every opportunity, and I was fortunate enough to be able to play along.

Such was the case on a brief stop in Qatar during a speaking tour in the Middle East. After an afternoon event in Doha, we were attending an informal dinner at the home of a sheik and his family prior to catching the evening flight for our next stop. Before the dinner, our hosts entertained us by showing us their horses. They also asked the General if he had ever been a falconer and, if not, whether he would like to be taught a bit of falconry.

In France, General Powell's autobiography was called *Un Enfant Du Bronx*, or *A Kid from the Bronx*, a title he readily embraced. He told the sheik that as a kid growing up in the inner city of New York, he had no experience with birds of prey. Laughingly, he offered me up as the bait, so to speak, to feed the birds. Within minutes, my arm was strapped in leather and raised to shoulder height, and I was told to stand very still: "Don't move a muscle." If the kid from the Bronx thought he had no experience (or interest) in communing with birds of prey, I have no idea why he thought this girl from the Virginia suburbs would be any better equipped for the "honor." With eyes squeezed shut and my breath held, I provided a perch for the comings and goings of a beautiful but heavy falcon with razor-like talons while General Powell, once again, had everyone laughing.

* * *

For various reasons, I didn't accompany the General for his engagement with a large trucking association's annual conference in Texas. As usual, though, I made all the preparations and managed the event logistics from my office, keeping close to the phone for status reports. Right on schedule, I received a call as General Powell got off the stage and was heading to the car I had arranged to take him to the airport for his next stop in Salt Lake City. When the phone rang, I immediately heard him say, "*Now, Leslie, don't worry.*"

When does anyone hear someone say, "*Now, don't worry,*" and *not* immediately start worrying?

During the Q&A session following his remarks, someone from the audience had asked him if, after all the General had accomplished in his life, there was anything he still wanted to do but never had.

"*Les, of course I was shameless and answered I had always wanted to drive an eighteen-wheeler.*"

He said that before the audience could stop laughing, a guy in the audience who owned a truck company stood up and promised to have an eighteen-wheeler waiting for him upon his arrival in Utah. General Powell tried to reassure me it probably wouldn't actually happen, but asked me to call the Governor of Utah's office with a warning "just in case," since the Governor or Lieutenant Governor and staff were expected to greet him at the airport and take him to an event.

As you have probably guessed, General Powell was welcomed at the airport by state and local officials, teams of security, and a very large red truck. Much to his delight, he got his wish and learned to drive the eighteen-wheeler on the service roads of the airport. He even got to honk the horn.

* * *

In early May of 2011, General Powell was asked by Scott Bohannon, an accomplished innovator in corporate leadership development, to participate in a roundtable discussion with a small group of clients of the Corporate Executive Board (later known as CEB Inc.). It was an engaging session with select executives having the unique opportunity to discuss crisis management, global politics, and current affairs. The fact that the General had appeared on several news programs discussing the discovery and death of Osama Bin Laden a couple days prior made the occasion especially memorable.

Despite the headiness of much of the discussion, the General was still able to share his natural bonhomie. Making a point about how the world is easily brought together with media coverage of international events, General Powell referenced Prince William's wedding to Kate Middleton which had also taken place that week. With a laugh, he challenged the assembled business leaders to admit that they had all gotten up hours before dawn just to watch the proceedings on television. "Come on! I know you did. Don't even try and deny it."

And then to emphasize the point, he pointed to me in the corner and said, "And I am sure Leslie watched it wearing a tiara while in pajamas."

Which was the perfect opening for my deadpan response, "Oh, please. Don't be silly. It was a color-coordinated hat. Anyone who is anyone knows it is gauche to wear a tiara before sunset."

* * *

As emcee of the 2014 Academy Awards, television talk show host Ellen DeGeneres famously took a star-studded selfie in front of the stage as part of the evening's televised celebration. It was a fun stunt and immediately went viral on social media.

Not to be outdone, as part of his "Throwback Thursday" tradition a few days later, General Powell posted on his Facebook page his version of a selfie he had taken in his mother's bedroom mirror as a teenager some sixty years prior claiming, "I was doing selfies 60 years before you Facebook folks. Eat your heart out, Ellen!"

We all were delighted when his posting made the national news.

* * *

In 2011, a magnitude 5.8 earthquake hit Virginia's Piedmont region. Although what I felt miles from the epicenter was mild, it was still unsettling to feel the earth move and see the resulting damage in the Washington, D.C., area.

Having lived all my life in Virginia, the only other quake I've ever experienced was several years later in Japan, after an engagement there with General Powell. On the night before our flight home, we were attending a small dinner with our hosts at a restaurant on the ground floor of a hotel skyscraper in downtown Tokyo. Just as the waitstaff began to clear the table of our first course, we heard the roar and felt the floor tremor beneath us. Without thinking, I jumped up from my seat and rushed over to the General, put my hands on his shoulders and announced, "That's an earthquake! I'll protect you!"

Earthquakes are a regular occurrence for Tokyo residents. Since buildings there (especially skyscrapers) are built to accommodate the earthquakes, no one else at the table seemed the least bit concerned. Consequently, General Powell responded, laughing, "Leslie! It's just an earthquake." And then turning to the guests, he said, "See what I have to put up with? She thinks she can hold up a building."

General Powell had a wonderful ability to inspire a smile or laugh even during trying times. As he was known to say, "Have a sense of humor to break the tension in times of great toil."

* * *

During a particularly busy time on the speaking circuit, we were getting ready for a week of back-to-back speeches across several states and one in Canada. The night before we were to fly to Chicago for the first event, he called to say, "*Les, there is nothing to worry about, but I tripped in the yard today. There is plenty of time before we fly tomorrow so just to be safe, I'll go up to Walter Reed and get them to take a look at my ankle.*"

The next phone call I received from him was from Walter Reed Military Medical Center, and the General admitted it was a bit more than "nothing to worry about," as his doctors had determined he had torn his Achilles tendon and his treatment required a walking cast boot. Nevertheless, he was determined to carry on with his engagements over the next few months. First though, we needed to make accommodations for the Chicago event later that day.

I called my contact and reassured him that we would arrive on schedule, but we needed a wheelchair and a ramp onto the stage. The client was concerned but I reassured him the General was only inconvenienced by his injury and would proceed as scheduled. Meanwhile, I worked with my charter plane contact to make sure all the FBOs (the charter plane hangars) had wheelchairs or golf carts and that my contracted cars had trunk space for crutches.

As his participation was a surprise for this group, the audience was not only astonished to hear who their keynote speaker was, but also to see the towering General being rolled in a wheelchair by his assistant (me) up the steep ramp onto the stage. I can't remember how he explained his injury, but he spun a tall tale of derring-do, leaving the audience in stitches once he fessed up that it was his own clumsiness in the backyard.

Our adventures of the torn Achilles tendon continued. Over the next few days, he had me scouting several big box stores in Northern Virginia for what he called a "swivel stool." Part of his mastery of any stage was his ability to walk around without being constrained by a lectern. With his injury, he would need to be propped onto something, and his solution was to get a bar stool that could spin him around, as this would be the best substitute for "walking the stage." So, off I went to a local Walmart, Target, and Sears, photographing and sending him pictures of stools. I can't remember how many I actually purchased and then returned before we found a small local chair company that had just what he wanted.

From that point on, everywhere we went, we carried his crutches and swivel stool. In that first week, we had a scheduled black-tie gala for the Jewish National Fund of Canada. For the VIP photo-op, he posed with all the leadership, sponsors, and families for pictures while perched astride his stool. I then steered his wheelchair through the crowds from the reception to the ballroom, parked the wheelchair, and gave him his crutches (which I'd been carrying under my arm) to help him to his seat at the head table. When time came for his keynote address, I led him through the reverse: crutches to wheelchair, wheelchair to stage, and crutches up onto the stage and swivel stool. This was especially challenging amidst a crowded ballroom of guests in black-tie. (Pre-event, he had figured out a way to squeeze his tuxedo slacks over his boot without having to cut it.)

All went well during the thoughtful and moving parts of his speech, while he had great fun bemoaning his one-legged maneu-verings. Departing the gala afterwards was a challenge though, especially given how hampered we were by all the accessories required by his injury. The ballroom had become uncomfortably warm by the end of the affair due to the large crowd, and we were happy to leave the heat behind. Once we got through the crowds, I wheeled his wheelchair down the long hall leading to the elevator. The picture on the front page of the newspaper the next day showed me looking like Nurse Ratchet from *One Flew Over the Cuckoo's Nest*, steering the wheelchair to the elevator with General Powell laughing with his host saying, "Faster, Leslie! Faster! Cool air on my face!"

Thankfully, soon after that engagement, the General found a knee scooter which allowed him to prop his lower leg on the bed of the scooter and wheel himself anywhere. As a joke, I went to a bicycle shop and purchased a metal trilling bell and one of those little squeeze horns kids put on their bike handles. Despite his initial reaction of, "You gotta be kidding me," he was soon shamelessly honking and ringing away. For the remaining weeks he was tethered to his scooter, if we didn't first see him coming, we certainly heard him. The boyish grin on his face as he zoomed past was something to behold and it was impossible not to laugh with him.

General Powell was known for many things. Ever the thoughtful military leader, dedicated diplomat, and inspirational speaker, he also had an incredible wit and knew how to engage an audience or anyone around him simply by playing for laughs. I was always delighted to play a sidekick, for it was the best seat in the house.

13.

Planting Seeds:
the Essence of Kindness

"Don't just show kindness in passing or to be courteous. Show it in depth, show it with passion, and expect nothing in return. Kindness is not just about being nice; it's about recognizing another human being who deserves care and respect."
—Colin Powell

I met General Powell after he retired from the army, but I can easily imagine the powerful effect his presence had on the young men and women serving under him. Though he was no longer in uniform, whenever we stopped at military posts, it was touching to see how "the troops" (as he always called them) gravitated toward him. He had a palpable commanding presence, and while he was an influential leader, he was also extremely kind. We would all do well to follow his example of sowing seeds of kindness wherever we are.

I'm always moved when I witness a young person's spontaneous reaction to being included in a significant moment. Such moments can move us to tears in an instant, but more importantly, they provide a memory we can recall for inspiration.

During the time General Powell was National Security Advisor, several years before I actually met him, I had the pleasure of escorting the Presidential Delegation, representing President Reagan, to Normandy, France, where they would participate in the celebrations commemorating the 44th anniversary of D-Day. As all members of the delegation under my care had to be approved by the National Security Council, the General had the final say in their selection. On the delegation's final night in France, we attended a parade and dinner given by the local townspeople in Sainte-Mère-Église. Buffet tables overflowed with delicious Norman cuisine; decorations included little toothpicks with the flags of England, Canada, France, and the United States, perched in cornichons and sausages; and standing guard amidst it all were hundreds of tiny plastic toy soldiers in WWII uniforms.

Serving our table was a young boy, not yet a teenager. He was a little shy and did not speak any English but was delighted when anyone from our delegation spoke to him in French. At the end of the evening, we tried our best to express our thanks to him for helping make the event special. One White House official had a pocketful of Presidential tchotchkes with Ronald Reagan's signature on them and he gave one to this young boy, who accepted it gravely, his blush plain to all. After saying our goodbyes, we watched him clutch his gift tightly in his hand as he turned and rushed into the outstretched arms of his dad, bursting into tears, overwhelmed by emotion.

Memories of that heartwarming moment came flooding back to me many years later while I was traveling with General Powell for a speech in Asia.

In April 2008, we traveled to China for the General to be a keynote speaker in the Boao Forum for Asia (BFA). Created in

2001, BFA is an annual pan-Asian meeting of government and business leaders to discuss key issues related to Asia and the world. For this three-day conference, over 1,700 international journalists and business and government leaders gathered in the scenic town of Boao in China's southern Hainan province. Chinese President Hu Jintao delivered the opening keynote speech, "Continuing Reform and Opening Up and Advancing Win-Win Cooperation." During the plenary session, General Powell delivered the closing keynote speech, "Sustainable Development, Sustainable Partnerships: Towards a Win-Win Future."

As with many international gatherings, we had our fair share of challenges. Our travel arrangements went well, but some on-site logistics were problematic. Sometimes there were last-minute changes required by political considerations. Other times the issues were those typical of many large-scale international gatherings, where language and cultural differences necessitate sensitive handling by an overwhelmed staff. Whatever their source, though, we were often frustrated. Fortunately, General Powell and I soon learned we could overcome every problem by relying on the young man assigned as our guide and official "babysitter," Guoyang Chen—or "Simon," as he told us to call him—a 20-year-old student in his freshman year at Hainan University.

Throughout our time in Hainan, Simon took care of our every need with cheerful efficiency. With quiet, deferential attention to every detail, Simon expertly shepherded us around many logistical and political obstacles. He was so successful, I almost felt sorry for the other international participants as we observed their frustration in dealing with the challenges we evaded thanks to Simon's deft maneuverings. Selfishly, we were glad he was ours alone and we didn't have to share him. Once we discovered Simon's magic touch, General Powell ignored the senior officials hosting the event whenever we ran into a roadblock and instead turned to and let Simon work his magic.

When we said our final goodbyes at the airport security gate before boarding our plane home, General Powell expressed his heartfelt gratitude to Simon for his expert help and steadfast support. Just before heading around the corner and out of sight, we turned around to wave and saw our Simon jumping up and down exuberantly, waving a final goodbye with tears running down his face.

Guoyang "Simon" Chen and I have remained in touch. When I mentioned to him in a direct message that I was writing this book and planned to mention our time together, he wrote back:

> It was one of the best memories of my life, and you may know that also it had a huge impact on my further education (thanks so much for writing the reference letter for my Master's applications) and career choice. You and the General showed me how the power of kindness can impact others, especially young people. I will cherish those three days of memories with you and General Powell for a life long (sic)."

Simon's thoughtful words are a wonderful reminder to all of us that a kindness given can also be a kindness received.

* * *

College campuses are often hotbeds of debate and the clash of ideas. On the speaking circuit, although we were aware of speakers sometimes encountering protests and counterprotests from various student groups, we rarely encountered any unrest requiring our special attention. Having always been a strong defender of the First Amendment, General Powell welcomed respectful debate.

At a large Midwestern university event in a basketball arena on campus, General Powell gave a stirring speech to a packed audience of students, faculty, and local community members. Unlike some speakers, General Powell never wanted to know questions in advance, so during the Q&A session that followed his remarks, he called on individuals directly from the audience, allowing them to ask whatever they wanted without screening.

As was often the case at that time, several questions were why he hadn't run for president, what it would take to convince him to run in the future, or some other attempt to ascertain or encourage future presidential aspirations.

He always handled these questions with good humor, accepting them as the compliments they were and answering definitively that running for office was not something he had "a fire in the belly" to pursue.

Amidst the wild acclaim of this very engaged and supportive audience, one young student took the microphone and began to lecture on a controversial subject, protesting the General's side of the issue. The audience quickly turned on the young man with boos and reproachful shouts in an attempt to silence him. With exceeding calm and admirable gentleness, General Powell calmed the crowd, "Let the young man speak." More importantly though, he reached out to the young man who was now visibly trembling in response to the crowd's punishing reaction, and said, "Son, please go on. You have a right to speak your mind."

Whatever the exact words were that General Powell used to answer the question, I'll only say he clearly expressed his opinion, which was contrary to the young man's stance, with a gentleness that saved the student from the ire of the crowd. General Powell's kindness was a clear command to the audience. By reiterating his steadfast protection of Freedom of Speech first, he'd gently chastised the crowd without even voicing a rebuke.

He often said, "Always show more kindness than seems necessary because the person receiving it needs it more than you will ever know."

* * *

When I first started working with the General, I remember being hesitant about revealing too much about myself. On one of our earliest long international flights together, somehow he broke his glasses and asked me to ask my counterpart at our destination to find a place to repair them or, alternatively, "You could always just loan me yours."

As my glasses were clearly a bit girly, it was obvious he was kidding. Even so, I remember taking a deep breath to reveal something I had not shared with him before: "*Ok, sure, but, uh... I should let you know, I wear glasses as a result of multiple sclerosis.*"

To which he simply said, "*Ok. So?*"

His nonchalant response was exactly what I needed. I had only had MS for a few years at that point, and it wasn't something I readily shared. By reacting as he would to any non-newsworthy announcement, he gave me the gift I hadn't realized I needed. And that acceptance was reassuring and I loved him for it.

* * *

It was a rare day when those of us in the General's world didn't receive multiple requests from people who all wanted something from him. The "asks," as we called them, covered everything from autographs to endorsements and appearances, and we received them both verbally and in writing. As I was aware of the volume of these daily requests, I tended to be hypersensitive and would cringe at the thought of friends or family ever even hinting they might want something. Although the General probably would not have minded, I was always cautious about ever adding yet another "ask" for him to consider.

In February 2016, General Powell was the keynote speaker at the Richmond Forum, a subscription speaker series that had been bringing world renowned leaders and celebrities to central Virginia for many years. As I am originally from Richmond, I have many relatives there. Consequently, I was delighted to purchase tickets for several of them to come hear "my" General speak in person. In addition, my forum contacts allowed me to invite them to the VIP reception following the speech.

In my desire to make sure my two aunts, two uncles, mother, and brother stayed in the background, I counseled them to enjoy the reception but to please not join the photo-op receiving line. I did not want to make the already long line of several hundred guests getting their pictures taken with the General any longer than it had to be.

I should have known better. As soon as we got through the seemingly endless line of guests, the General turned to me and barked, "*Lautenslager, where d'you hide your family? Get 'em.*" He knew I'd likely admonished them to stay in the background and away from the photographer. With a twinkle in his eye, he over-ruled me and gathered them all for a quick group photo. When

I tried to stay out of it, he made me hop into the middle. Bless him, despite my plans to keep my family from prolonging the event, his simple kindness produced a photograph still treasured by my family.

* * *

There is a proverb that originated in the region of southern Africa and reads in the Zulu language, "*Umuntu ngumuntu ngabantu.*" This is the core tenant of the philosophy of Ubuntu which means, "*I am because we are.*" In other words, to be human is to recognize the humanity of others. When we are in harmony with our humanity, our *ubuntu*, even the most daunting problems can be resolved as we recognize the basic dignity in everyone else. *Unbuntu* is a belief that there is a universal bond connecting us all.

This spirit of Ubuntu well describes what I observed during a trip to Colorado for one of the General's speaking engagements. Rather than return home immediately after his speech, General Powell was asked to visit both a juvenile detention center and the juvenile offenders' section of a state penitentiary. The state officials who invited him hoped a few minutes with the incarcerated teenaged boys in each place might leave a positive impression.

This was the first time I had ever set foot inside a prison. The experience was sobering, and I can't fully describe how it felt to be in the room when General Powell addressed those boys. Many had committed serious crimes and were serving long sentences, but some would be free to start new lives in a few years. Regardless, General Powell addressed them as he would have any other group—with dignity and respect for the humanity in each of them. He acknowledged their present circumstances and didn't sugarcoat their reality or downplay the seriousness of what they'd done to be there. Nevertheless, he hammered home his oft-quoted admonition, "None of us can change our yesterdays but all of us can change our tomorrows."

Later in the car, I confessed how moved I was by his interactions with those young men. In his typical straightforward way, he admitted there was little reason to hope for many of them. Nonetheless, he reminded me that whenever there is a chance one's effort might make a difference to someone struggling, we must take it.

His message was humbling, encouraging, and profound.

Throughout junior high and high school, my theater teachers, Miss Wilburn and Mr. Westlake, often quoted Constantin Stanislavski, the world-renowned Russian actor and theatre director, saying, "There are no small parts, only small actors." As a young eager thespian, this was a good reminder to treat my assigned part as important no matter how few lines I had or how little time I was on stage.

The General may never have quoted Stanislavski, but he certainly modeled the concept of embracing service no matter the role. Following the Presidents' Summit for America's Future in 1997, America's Promise Alliance (APA) was launched and chaired by General Powell. APA's efforts and initiatives focus on providing resources that all children need to grow into successful adults. These needs are described as the Five Promises:

1. Caring adults in their lives to guide and encourage them;

2. Safe places, both physical and psychological,
   in which children can safely develop;

3. A healthy start in life (including, among other things, proper nutrition, exercise, and medical care)

4. Effective education that prepares them for work and life; and

5. Opportunities to serve and help others.

In launching America's Promise Alliance in 1997, General Powell reminded us all at the National Service Summit:

> This is about Americans getting off the sidelines and getting onto the playing field. This is about each and every one of us who have been blessed by the wealth of this country sharing that blessing by reaching down and reaching back and lifting up somebody in need. That's what America is about. That's what being American is all about.

The General had a way with words and perhaps no quote of his better than this one captures the belief that we all have a responsibility and the ability to help young people:

> All children need a laptop. Not a computer, but a human laptop. Moms, Dads, Grannies and Grandpas, Aunts, Uncles— someone to hold them, read to them, teach them. Loved ones who will embrace them and pass on the experience, rituals, and knowledge of a hundred previous generations. Loved ones who will pass to the next generation their expectations of them, their hopes, and their dreams.

Serving as APA chairman until he became Secretary of State, General Powell provided leadership for the organization on a national scale. He supported its mission closer to home as well. One of his many efforts included initiating a partnership between St. John's Episcopal, his local church in the Virginia suburbs, and an inner-city middle school in Washington, D.C. With significant tutoring and development programs, this partnership allowed members of his church to foster strong positive relationships with students from his "adopted" school.

A school program that was particularly effective was the Colin L. Powell Leadership Club. During meetings of this afterschool club, students were provided encouragement to do well in school and enrichment opportunities to learn about careers and life skills from successful adults. General Powell met occasionally with the students and encouraged colleagues and friends to do so as well.

It was always a pleasure to join the St. John's team of tutors and be a guest speaker at one of the club meetings each year, although keeping energetic preteens and young teenagers engaged could be a challenge. On these occasions, I would teach a class on "Protocol 101," emphasizing how small the world is and how important it is to appreciate cultural differences. As part of my attempt to demystify a sometimes-intimidating concept, each time I would compare protocol to being kind and respectful when getting to know people and developing friendships. Seeing several of the children then clearly understand my example was a joy and something I happily reported to the General, eager to share the fruits of my labors by following his example.

At the end of the school year each summer, General and Mrs. Powell welcomed the club members to their house for a pool party. While I helped Frank Branch, the Powells' houseman, flip burgers for the hungry middle-schoolers, General Powell could always be seen teaching a child, whether by showing one who had never been in a pool before how to swim, or giving gentle counsel to children eager to spend time with him.

* * *

While working on an official visit to the United States of a senior Chinese leader early in my career, I was part of the team coordinating his visit to Minnesota, where the delegation would spend time with the Twin Cities Chinese community. To welcome the leader upon his arrival in Minneapolis, a distinguished group of local VIPs was arranged along the red carpet from the plane to the motorcade. With every formality and courtesy in place, I was to escort a little Chinese-American girl to the foot of the red carpet so that she could present a bouquet of flowers to the leader on behalf of the local Chinese-American community. That was it. My only job, my only assignment for the welcome ceremony, was to hold the hand of a sweet little five-year old on the red carpet and then return her to her parents.

I confess being disappointed I wasn't tasked with a more glamorous job than being what I perceived as nothing more than just a babysitter. What made that experience memorable though decades later, and in the context of Stanislavski's words of wisdom and General Powell's example, was what happened after the motorcade left. As all the VIPs dispersed, the little girl's mother came over to tell me what her daughter had whispered in her ear but was too shy to tell me herself. The little girl wanted me to know that when she grew up, she hoped she could be just like me.

Wherever my career and adventures have taken me since, I have always treasured that little girl's gift—a reminder that no matter what an individual's part is in the bigger picture, it is important because it can always make a difference to others.

Such was the case on the road with General Powell. Not so much for security reasons but rather to take advantage of the fastest ways to avoid crowds, we would enter and exit hotels and convention centers through back hallways, kitchens, and loading docks. Keeping on schedule was much easier this way and these evasive maneuvers allowed the General to cross paths with those who worked out of the spotlight. Witnessing their reaction to his hello and thank you, often in the language of the person crossing his path, or seeing their delight in shaking his outstretched hand was a treat. Even better was watching them laugh when he'd try and steal a cookie while exiting the kitchens.

* * *

While General Powell was in the White House as the National Security Advisor, I, as part of my duties as a Department of State protocol visits officer, was assigned to take care of the private visits to the United States of His Excellency José Napoleón Duarte, President of El Salvador. As a chief of state, President Duarte's visits to the U.S. were often official visits with all the requisite White House, State Department and congressional meetings and functions. However, he also traveled often to Washington, D.C. for very quiet private visits, since he was undergoing treatment for advanced stomach cancer at Walter Reed Army Medical Center. Whenever I arrived with his motorcade at the Medical Center, I was always relieved when I could hand him over to his medical team.

Following a particularly difficult cancer treatment, President Duarte's motorcade arrived on the flight line for his flight home and he had to be taken to the plane by wheelchair. When it became apparent that he was too weak even to climb the few steps into the plane, one of the pilots gently draped the President of El Salvador's arms over his shoulders and carried him on his back into the plane. Although each of us did everything we could to allow President Duarte as much dignity as we could, my heart still hurts remembering that moment, and I hope each of us there helped make the difficult situation as painless, both literally and figuratively, as possible.

*　　*　　*

General Powell delighted in visiting the various military bases in the Washington, D.C. area. If someone wanted to stand in line to buy his book, he would laugh and say he would certainly be happy to sign it. This was in addition to the hundreds of thousands of bookplates he signed, never auto-penned. Many laughs were shared with those who waited for the chance to have their books signed, their picture taken, and maybe even a baby kissed. Sometimes those coming through the lines were soldiers with catastrophic injuries suffered in Afghanistan or Iraq. The General always shared a few extra moments with them and would later say that more than sympathy, they most welcomed his interest in where they'd served and his appreciation for their families.

Similarly, during every PBS televised National Memorial Day Concert, we could witness General Powell greeting the survivors or family members of those who had been recognized from the stage. Despite not hearing his words televised, it was obvious the

General's presence provided comfort. And he provided an example we would all do well to follow.

* * *

Throughout the pandemic, my world was colored by the fact I was constantly around three octogenarians I loved dearly—my mother, the General, and Mrs. Powell—and every decision I made on a daily basis considered their well-being. Unfortunately, my beloved Uncle Jim, my mother's brother, James Duke, died of COVID-19 within weeks after the pandemic started. Like the experience of so many during those early days, we suffered the heartache of being unable to gather with family and friends to comfort one another and celebrate the loved one's life.

Aside from COVID-19's challenges, during this period the realities of age and the passage of time were constant reminders that life is short. Whether by phone or in person in "the Bunker," General Powell and I had many sad conversations about the passing of yet another friend or relative. He was always quick to reach out in sympathy and with encouragement to those he knew were suffering and experiencing tremendous loss.

A kind word from General Powell was always a gift and a reminder to pass it on. As he always said, "Treat people kindly. When you are kind to somebody, and I don't mean necessarily buddy-buddy, just show kindness and consideration. Show that people are worthy and you respect them and you are glad they're with you."

14.

When Mourning
Becomes Responsibility

"I have the deepest regret about 9/11. September 11, 2001, was one of the most difficult days I've ever had. I was in Lima, Peru, and had to fly back eight hours not knowing what happened in my own country, knowing thousands of my fellow citizens had died."
—Colin Powel, "News Hour with Jim Lehrer," 26 March 2004

"You can be sure that the American spirit will prevail over this tragedy."
—Colin Powell, "Special General Assembly of the Organization of American States,"

11 September 2001

One of the most profound theater experiences I have ever experienced was watching a production of the Broadway hit, "Come From Away." This wonderful musical tells the story of the small Canadian town in Newfoundland that welcomed nearly 6,700 travelers when their planes were forced to land in Gander as the result of the terror attacks of 9/11. The townspeople welcomed people from around the world—or as Newfoundlanders call them, the "come from aways"—as guests.

The stranded passengers came from dozens of different countries, ranging from Austria to the United Arab Emirates, and from nearly every state in the U.S.

Days after seeing the production, I read a review in *USA Today* which included a beautiful description of what the townspeople provided their unexpected guests: "an oasis of kindness."

An oasis of kindness.

What a wonderful description of what we all should be willing to provide. Shouldn't we all offer a soft landing for others when they're faced with adversity or heartbreak?

In late April 1999, a couple days prior to General Powell taking part in back-to-back engagements, I was grocery shopping for a murder mystery dinner party I was hosting when my cell phone rang. Actually, it vibrated, as I never allow the ringer to be audible in public places. When I saw in the phone screen the call was from the General, I immediately answered.

His call put everything else I was doing in perspective and on hold. General Powell had just been asked to join Vice President Al Gore and Colorado Governor Bill Owens for the memorial service honoring the students and teacher who were killed on April 20th in the Columbine High School massacre. Would I, he asked, immediately make new travel arrangements that would allow us to stop in Littleton, Colorado, in order for him to participate in the April 25th service before continuing onto his already scheduled speaking engagements?

Although he was not being asked to speak during the program, those planning the event knew having General Powell among the many leaders there was important. They believed the

General's presence on the dais and meeting with the grieving families and members of the Columbine community would be reassuring and comforting.

I made the appropriate arrangements and when our plane arrived in Colorado, we were met by state officials eager to welcome General Powell. As we were being escorted to the motorcade, I was an unforgiving gatekeeper. One of the ranking state leaders who was soon up for reelection had an overly eager staffer there trying desperately to get a photograph of his boss walking beside the General. I overheard him say he was anxious to get a clean shot so it could be used as a campaign photo. Without uttering a word, I made sure I was always positioned to block his view. There is a time and place for everything, but allowing a political campaign to benefit from a photo with the General at such a somber occasion seemed unconscionable. I can only hope the young man has gained some perspective over time.

The event was held in the parking lot of a local shopping mall, the largest available space in the area, to accommodate the expected crowds. Despite the rain throughout the afternoon, approximately 80,000 people gathered and mourned together. Vice President Gore, Governor Owens, other officials, and religious leaders spoke words of comfort while singer-songwriters Amy Grant and Michael W. Smith provided inspirational music. The most moving parts of the program, though, were shared by the students from Columbine who sang songs they had written in memory of their classmates.

It was a powerful and moving service. Although there is no way to alleviate the pain and suffering that comes from tragedies such as Columbine, being there provided the ministry of presence—something we each can do when others grieve.

* * *

In March 2006, when former Secretary of Defense Caspar "Cap" Weinberger died, General Powell delivered a eulogy for his dear friend. During that same week, I attended funerals celebrating the life of a cousin and the life of a former boss. At times, it seems when it rains it pours, and so it was that week. While the General spent long hours preparing for the remarks he would deliver honoring his friend, I was reminded of a piece I'd written for a friend to be used for a national day of mourning observance, which I'd titled "Protocol for Remembrance." With all the two of us were facing that week, I felt compelled to share it with the General. Much like any student who wants to please a teacher, I often shared my efforts with him, not for instructional purposes, but because I simply wanted to share my thoughts, knowing they often reflected recurring themes of his.

From my "Protocol for Remembrance," which I have shared several times with international protocol colleagues:

In all you do and in all you say, be kind.

Being human means we all at some point experience the death of loved ones as well as bear witness to the death of others we do not know. In protocol, we even are sometimes asked to plan and assist with memorial services for officials and dignitaries. Let us be reminded how our every gesture, word, and deed during days of remembrance can be gently chosen to best serve the grieving as well as be reverent for the occasion.

Remember offering a simple word of sympathy and condolence to anyone who grieves can be comforting. Please don't be fearful that you don't know the "right" words... There are no right words.

Sharing a kind word to show you care is enough.

Whether for funerals of loved ones or for memorial services on a national or international stage, sober dress is always most appropriate. Although gone are the days where all mourning attire had to be black, it is still considered best to dress in a fashion that reflects the somberness of the occasion and in a way that does not cause offense to those grieving.

Sometimes the "ministry of presence"—where no word is spoken—is the kindest gift of all to those in mourning. Simply standing by a loved one, a friend, a colleague, and sometimes, even most especially, a stranger, is often all the appropriate comfort necessary.

In attending remembrance services, like attending funerals, respect the traditions of the occasion even when the traditions and culture may not be your own.

Protocol of any situation often entails knowing and following many rules. Be mindful, though, that underlying even the strictest and most formally choreographed memorial or funeral service is always the very basic need to reach out to those who mourn with a simple protocol for remembrance that can be summed up simply as "be kind."

* * *

When former President Reagan died, General Powell and I were in Normandy, France for the celebration of the 60th anniversary of D-Day. Although he was attending in his official capacity as Secretary of State, I was there as a private citizen. Having worked and lived in Normandy during the five years I was Director of Special Events and Protocol for the Battle of Normandy Foundation, before meeting the General, I was attending the ceremonies with my beloved adopted French families.

On the morning of June 6th, I woke up early in order to make it to the official ceremony at the U.S. Cemetery. I was staying with Corinne Marquet, my French "sister," and her husband, Julien, and as soon as we greeted each other that morning she shared a radio announcement that President Reagan had just died. Two things immediately came to mind—one that was tremendously moving, and one that was tremendously sobering. The timing of his death was just a day shy of the anniversary of his "These Are the Boys of Point du Hoc" speech, given during the 40th Anniversary of D-Day commemorations in 1984, a moving speech that still brings tears to my eyes each time I hear or even think of it.

On a practical level, though, the news kick-started me into professional mode. In my role as Assistant Chief of Protocol, I attended meetings every few months with officials throughout the government—from the White House, the Capitol, all the various law enforcement agencies, the Military District of Washington, National Cathedral, etc.—to plan state funerals. Although it was always an unnamed president's funeral we were planning, we were pretty certain Ronald Reagan's service would be the most likely to come next. A state funeral is a tremendously important protocol event, and there is a finite time frame within which to work: from the moment of death up to the burial is only seven days. Because Ronald Reagan served at a unique point in history and was revered by many world leaders, we knew his funeral would be unique.

General Powell as Secretary of State would be traveling home with the official U.S. delegation, but I would be flying on a commercial airline. My flight home was already scheduled for June 7th, so even though I needed to return from Europe as soon as possible, there was no way to get back any sooner than my confirmed ticketed flight. After the memorial ceremonies of June 6th,

I called my mother with explicit instructions and questions to pass along to my staff. I called her that morning knowing that, as "Mom Margaret" to my staff, she would have been hearing from my colleagues throughout the day and would be the most efficient point person for me to relay information to. (Mind you, this was in 2004, before ubiquitous cell phones and text messaging.) She confirmed my staff needed me to go directly to the office from the airport as soon as I arrived the next evening.

Preparing for any state funeral requires working almost around the clock, and this one was going to require every last minute. Many of the invited world leaders were already in the United States at that time, attending the G7 meeting in Georgia, and many former world leaders were also planning to attend the funeral. (For many years, former United Kingdom Prime Minister Margaret Thatcher always traveled with a black suit in her suitcase so that she would be ready no matter where she was if and when she learned of her dear friend Ronnie's passing.) In addition to all the government officials involved, Rick Ahearn (whom I previously mentioned had first brought me into General Powell's world) and Shelby Scarbrough were in charge of Mrs. Reagan's and the family's plans for the funeral.

Once I was back in D.C., we all dove into the work we'd long been training to do. Preparations were underway on Capitol Hill for the lying in state, and arrangements were well in hand at the National Cathedral for the service there. One portion of the event was still in limbo, however. Would the President of the United States host something at the White House following the funeral service?

There is a tradition, especially in the South, of holding a reception of some kind immediately following a funeral service.

Would we at the State Department need to host something for the international dignitaries, or would the White House do it? It would be one or the other, not both. We already knew that in addition to all the living former U.S. presidents, there would be eighty-two chiefs of state, heads of government, and foreign ministers attending, along with the diplomatic corps.

We knew, too, that former leaders Margaret Thatcher from the U.K., Helmut Kohl from Germany, Mikhail Gorbachev from Russia, Brian Mulroney from Canada, and Crown Prince Charles of the U.K. would also attend. To top it all off, immediately following the service at the National Cathedral, the former president's body would need to be flown on Air Force One from Andrews Air Force Base to California. At the same time, President Bush and others would be flying out of Andrews to attend the 80th birthday celebrations of his father, former President George H.W. Bush, in Houston. This meant the airspace over Washington, D.C., would be shut down for several hours, marooning all these world leaders in Washington until the airspace was cleared.

Secretary Powell and I were on email communication throughout the day while we waited for guidance from the White House. A day and a half before the scheduled funeral, when he finally got word that President Bush would not be hosting a reception to receive the leaders following the service, Secretary Powell called and asked me to come up to his office and bring whomever else I needed to discuss what to do following the funeral. I summoned April Guice from my staff and Larry Dunham, Assistant Chief of Protocol for Diplomatic Affairs, to come with me to meet with the Secretary of State, the Deputy Secretary Rich Armitage, and Under Secretary for Management Grant Green—exceptional public servants all. The Secretary shared what he'd learned from the White House. It put the responsibility on us to plan an event for some of the most powerful past and present world leaders—in less than 48 hours.

We discussed how to deal with having so many world leaders "stranded" in Washington after the funeral and all options were on the table. We knew it would be appropriate if not imperative for our distinguished guests to be offered some kind of hospitality. After several minutes of serious discussion, Secretary Powell turned to me and asked simply, "Leslie, can you do it?"

We held eye contact and I knew he was giving me unspoken permission to say no. But he knew there was no way I would say anything but what I did: "Yes, we can do it, and we will."

It was just like when he had turned to me before the ceremony expanding NATO: this was one of the most memorable moments in my years with him at the State Department. The fact that he had confidence in me—or rather in my team and me—to do something of this import with so little time was deeply affecting. There was no way we would let him down.

Much to our relief, all the logistics of the service went well. Each of the competing motorcades arrived as planned and the guests were appropriately seated. As the Chief of Protocol was stationed to greet the arrival of the motorcades, I was tasked to "babysit" the Dean of the Diplomatic Corps, so I was seated beside Ambassador of Saudi Arabia Prince Bandar, the senior ranking ambassador at that time. Our section for the Diplomatic Corps was situated immediately behind that reserved for members of the Supreme Court, or as we called them, "the Supremes."

Our seating was near the entrance where the leaders entered, and I will forever remember Prince Bandar's words to me as Mikhail Gorbachev passed us, "I hope you appreciate this moment. Surely,

Ronnie is looking down at us from heaven smiling and saying, 'Isn't this a wonderful world? Gorby, the leader of the evil empire is here at my funeral as a friend.'" Prince Bandar continued, "And furthermore, immediately after the funeral is over, I am flying Gorbachev on my plane for Bush Forty-One's 80th birthday celebration in Houston."

The funeral was appropriate for a leader of President Reagan's renown, with eulogies both heartwarming and profound. The reception we held afterwards at the Department of State was one fit for leaders and members of the diplomatic corps. While Secretary and Mrs. Powell greeted guests in the Benjamin Franklin Room on the 8th floor, Deputy Secretary of State Rich Armitage greeted the leaders and ambassadors as they arrived at the entrance of the State Department.

I can't adequately describe how profound the memorial service was. The funeral was a significant international event, but the reception we hosted on behalf of Secretary and Mrs. Powell was a marvel. My protocol colleagues, the Diplomatic Reception Rooms staff, the Diplomatic Security officers, and the caterer, all ensured the post-funeral event was flawless, and I will be forever grateful.

*　*　*

Although chronologically, the Reagan state funeral occurred years after, I choose to end this chapter with reflections on 9/11 and the fraught weeks that followed. Our world changed on that day, and although my experiences pale in comparison to those who were more directly affected, I offer my meager words as just one tiny testament to those horrible days.

During our many years together, whenever General Powell

and I were not traveling together, each time one of us arrived at our destination we would call the other to say "I've arrived safe and sound, all is well." It may sound silly, but it was a tradition we established over the years and followed religiously. When either one of us was tardy in our report, the other would tease mercilessly, saying something like, "Sigh. Once again, unloved and forgotten."

Such was the case on the morning of September 11th. Shortly after 8:00 am, Secretary Powell had just arrived in Lima, Peru, and called my bat line with "*Hi, Babycake, whadyasay?*" I responded with my normal laundry list of everything happening in my world—in this case, reminding him of our preparations for the Prime Minister of Australia's visit and address to the joint meeting of Congress the next day, as well as of my staff packing up to move to New York for several weeks for the annual opening of the United Nations General Assembly. Although I don't remember my exact words, I know I ended my conversation with a wish for good luck and admonitions to stay safe and do good.

Moments later, the world changed.

I do not have the words to describe what happened that day. From my perspective, the heartbreak was indescribable. Before we could even see it on the news, a colleague received a call from a carpool member who, from her window on the 7th floor of the State Department, saw the Pentagon explode in flames as the plane crashed into it. Moments later, the Deputy Chief of Protocol ran into our office suite, slammed my door, got down on his knees, and asked me to pray with him. A very short time later, Assistant Chief of Protocol Spencer Geissinger burst through the door from the hall shouting we needed to get out of the building immediately.

Our evacuation was surreal. Washington, D.C. became an island: all the bridges were closed, as no one knew where the terrorists might hit next. My normally 45-minute commute became a 3-hour nightmare. As I drove just a few hundred yards away, plumes of fire and smoke rose from the Pentagon and obscured most of my view. Only later did I learn that a childhood friend, Dave Laychek, was among the many who'd perished there.

Despite the horror of the day, I have never experienced a kinder commute. The driver in every car I drove beside was eager to let another pass even to get just a little further along the road as we all drove with tears streaming down our faces. I kept telling myself that if I could just get as far as the Washington Speakers Bureau, halfway between the State Department and my home, I would be ok. I knew if I could get that far, Bernie Swain and Harry Rhoads would welcome me into the WSB offices and allow me to crawl into a corner and cry. In the end, I didn't really have to stop and I made it home, but that reassurance kept me going.

After we were evacuated that Tuesday, even before we could return to our offices, we went into official mode, canceling everything related to the Prime Minister of Australia's official visit. Simultaneously, since President Bush announced that Friday would be a National Day of Prayer with a prayer service at the Washington National Cathedral, we began issuing invitations to all the foreign ambassadors. As with all national ceremonies, the Office of Protocol hosts and shepherds the diplomatic corps to attend large events such as this. This time, unlike many a "Dip Corps" event, few ambassadors would regret the invitation. Each respective foreign ministry would mandate attendance as a sign of solidarity.

On Friday morning, we gathered the ambassadors at the State Department for the requisite security check prior to boarding the security-swept buses for transport to the Cathedral. While assembling everyone, we provided light refreshments and shared information about the anticipated program.

Like so many people that week, we were operating mostly on autopilot. It was a difficult tightrope as we flitted about tending to our guests while dealing with our own individual and collective grief. Amidst this flurry, the Ambassador of Uganda, of whom I was quite fond reached out and grabbed both of my hands, bringing my busyness to a halt. The ambassador held on tightly, looked into my eyes and gently chastised, "Leslie, stop! Just stop. You can cry. You can cry because we are all crying with you. The world is crying with you. Stop. It's ok. You can cry."

Truly an oasis of kindness.

When we got to the Cathedral, the sky was overcast and a light rain was falling. We escorted the diplomats to their seats, and though the aisles were lit, the gray sky outside left the interior bathed in a somber light. Cathedral volunteers disbursed programs along with little red, white, and blue ribbons—a patriotic badge many of the ambassadors eagerly accepted. Prince Bandar, Dean of the Diplomatic Corps, resplendent in the robes of his national dress, asked, "Leslie, would you do me the honor of pinning one on me?" This was a significant gesture—as a female and a foreigner, I was being allowed to gently bypass traditional protocol in acknowledgement of the current circumstances.

The service was powerful. Clergy from many different faith traditions spoke prior to President Bush's address. The music was beautiful and during the final hymn, two remarkable things happened. As anyone who has tried to sing while trying not to cry knows, the sound is strained at best. During the first verses of the hymn, the song from the congregation was cacophonous. Somehow though, by the last verse, the blended voices sounded as if angels were singing, and by the end of the song the sun broke through the clouds and we were bathed in rainbow colors streaming through the Cathedral's stained-glass windows. It was a breathtaking yet gentle reminder we would get through this.

On Saturday morning, my brother Win and I were desperately trying to fix a flag pole in the front yard and as I was trying to keep the flag from touching the ground, I had it resting over my shoulders. At that moment, I finally received a call from Secretary Powell calling from Camp David. Although he and I had emailed and texted often throughout the week, we had not actually spoken with each other since that phone call from Lima.

Standing there in the sunshine, draped in the American flag, I finally had a chance to speak with him voice to voice, and I was overcome with relief. I also went right into mother hen mode, asking if he were eating and sleeping. I was worrying for naught, as he reminded me that from his earliest days as a First Lieutenant, "*As they taught us at Ft. Benning, I know to always eat and sleep whenever possible.*" Barely stopping to catch my breath, I asked if the President were eating and sleeping. He reassured me there were plenty of people, including the First Lady, making sure he was ok as well. It wasn't a long conversation, but I was comforted just hearing his voice. Just before saying goodbye, he reassured me, "*We will get through this.*"

* * *

After the death of a national leader or following a national tragedy, embassies around the world open condolence books, allowing members of the public to sign and offer words of sympathy during a declared period of mourning. Afterwards, these books of condolence are sent to the Office of Protocol at the Department of State—and specifically to my office suite.

For 9/11 though, our embassies not only collected hundreds of thousands of pages of signatures, but countless boxes of items left by people expressing their condolences in other symbolic ways. We received teddy bears and handmade quilts for children and families of firefighters and first responders who died, and thousands of origami peace doves made by elementary school children in Japan. There were murals painted by First Nation children in Canada, and drawings and letters in a multitude of languages, among so many other kind gestures. Within weeks, we were surrounded by boxes stacked floor to ceiling from all over the world.

My office maintained an "information line" which members of the public could call with protocol related questions. For instance, the mayor of Boise's office staff might call wanting to know how to address the mayor of Berlin during an upcoming meeting. Similarly, we might hear from a university's communications office wanting to know in what order they should post the flags of their international students. In one book by Letitia Baldridge, the late etiquette expert even directed readers with questions on international business etiquette to call a specific phone number—which rang on my desk. Although anyone on my staff could answer that line, I often enjoyed taking the calls myself.

On one of those early days after 9/11, when the info line rang, I took a call from the owner of a car dealership somewhere in the Midwest. This gentleman explained he needed guidance on what to do about his flag. President Bush had designated that the nation's flags would be flown at half-staff for 30 days. My caller explained he understood flag protocol dictated that a flag can only be flown at night if properly illuminated, but otherwise must be retired each day at sunset. Unfortunately, he admitted he didn't have the means to keep his flag lit at night. At this point, his voice broke as he stifled a sob. He continued with difficulty, saying he simply couldn't bring himself to bring the flag down each night, as his community needed to see that flag flying night and day. *"Please,"* he pleaded, *"what should I do?"*

At that point, the caller was unable to talk at all. Although my staff couldn't hear what was said on the phone, because I was now sobbing too, they gathered close and were in tears as well.

Normally I would quote chapter and verse on how to properly display a flag in adherence to night and weather restrictions. At that moment, however, I took a deep breath and marshaled whatever voice of authority I could before slamming my fist down on my desk, declaring, "Sir, you fly that flag! You tell anyone who asks that Washington, D.C. says you can fly that flag no matter what flag protocol says. You fly that flag for your community and for all of us. God bless America. We will get through this."

And truly, the best thing I could share in that moment with my newfound phone friend was Secretary Powell's message to me from days before:

"We will get through this."

15.

Joy and Sorrow

"February 5, 2003, the day of the speech, is as burned into my memory as my own birthday."
— Colin L. Powell, "It Worked For Me," p. 217

"As we move on, we must make sure the lessons learned are never forgotten or ignored."
— Colin L. Powell, "It Worked For Me," p. 224

Friends know me as someone who sees life through rose-colored glasses and avoids controversy whenever possible. Nevertheless, I need to address the proverbial elephant in the room. To avoid that topic would be naïve and leave this story, the General's and mine, incomplete.

In his book, *The Prophet,* Kahlil Gibran explores the dichotomy of joy and sadness in the poetic essay, *"On Joy and Sorrow."* Through his lyrical imagery, he describes the juxtaposition of the two seemingly opposite emotions as interconnected and says that in life we will inevitably experience both.

I remember the week of my 40th birthday as one of great joy but also one forever colored in history by sadness and regret.

General Powell and I celebrated each other's birthdays in various ways over the years. I always had fun trying to figure out something unique to give the guy who had multiples of everything, often settling on something silly that I knew would make him laugh. I was as easily entertained by the quest as I was figuring out creative ways to wrap and present the gift. As for the General's surprises for me, they were always sweet and thoughtful, though usually barely wrapped, with a simply scrawled sharpie sentiment across the top.

I turned 40 years old on Wednesday, February 5, 2003. The day was filled with all sorts of celebrations. My Ceremonials staff at the State Department surprised me with a delicious sheet cake adorned with a baby picture of me in icing across the top. (Note to all who have cakes like this, there is a natural hesitancy to actually eat the baby. In the end, we chose to "retire" the final pieces of cake rather than eat that little dimpled face.) The rest of the Office of Protocol sang to me while making me dance for the camera with the Deputy Chief of Protocol. Later that afternoon, my mother surprised me with a mother/daughter tea, inviting mothers and daughters from every decade of my life. Ending the day was the traditional birthday dinner my mother, my brother, and I share on each other's birthday.

When I first got to my desk that morning though, the "Bat Phone" rang. As soon as I uttered "Good morning," Secretary Powell jumped into singing "Happy Birthday" at full volume to me from New York.

Once the song and our laughter ended, we chatted briefly about the day's schedule. I knew the previous four days had been difficult for him and his senior staff as they prepared for the speech he was to give at the President's behest to the United Nations Security

Council. His presentation was meticulously constructed after analyzing every detail provided by the intelligence communities. It had been a stressful few days getting ready and I gave him my best wishes and a "break a leg" admonition for luck as I said goodbye.

Late that evening, the day concluded as it always did, with our signing off with a final goodnight (a routine which we called our "night-night" note, or simply "nn"). I congratulated him on how his day had seemed to go at the U.N., and he shared an additional birthday congratulations.

My birthday celebrations that week were to end Saturday night with a small dinner party at the home of my dear college friends, Mary and Mark Forde. I say "small," as I had agreed to no more than a half dozen or so guests. Because a heavy snowstorm hit Washington, D.C. a couple days before, there were moments we worried we would have to cancel. Fortunately, the roads cleared enough that I was able to drive to their home in the dark safely.

As soon as I knocked on the door, Mary swung it open and I was overwhelmed with joyous shouts of "*Surprise!*" from many more than the half dozen guests I was expecting. Besides old college friends, I saw uncles, aunts, and cousins from Richmond, former bosses and childhood friends, along with my mother and brother. For the next twenty minutes, I had great fun greeting everyone and sharing how much their presence meant to me. Their smiles however, hid the secret of an additional surprise still to come.

I'm not sure who called out first but several voices could be heard gleefully telling me to go back to the front door for a final arrival. And with that, I turned in sight of the entrance and was floored to see the Secretary of State and Mrs. Powell arrive for this special birthday celebration.

Protocol professionals are familiar with the security details that often accompany government officials and important dignitaries. We know how and when to make accommodations to adapt to security requirements, and although the process is usually painless, sometimes the requirements can be extensive. When a "sweep" is required (i.e., when bomb sniffing dogs are brought in to sweep a facility), all arrangements and setups must be completed well in advance.

This is all standard operating procedure in my professional world and pretty much taken for granted. It's not so normal for friends and family outside my working world though. Such was the case for Mary and Mark. In the days leading up to the party, they'd quickly become experts in knowing how to prep their house and neighborhood for the arrival of the world's top diplomat.

Despite a snowstorm and his having been in New York at the U.N. on my actual birthday three days before, my beloved General as Secretary of State made it to the party——and timed it on purpose to arrive after I did. Had he not, the surprise of my walking up to the house expecting nothing more than a small dinner party would have been blown, as I would have seen the armed US Diplomatic Security team surrounding my friends' house with dogs and bulletproof vehicles—with motors running in case of the need for a quick getaway.

I treasure a black and white candid photo from that night: It's of Secretary Powell, head thrown back in laughter, his arms around me in a tight bear hug as I hide my face in his chest. Mrs. Powell and Ambassador Roosevelt can be seen over our shoulders laughing in delight. It was a joyful moment for everyone there.

In General Powell's book, *It Worked For Me*, Chapter 35 is titled simply, "February 5, 2003 – The United Nations." In the chapter, he addresses the difficult speech preparation and delivery as well as the painful repercussions that followed when it was eventually determined by the Iraq Intelligence Commission, created by presidential executive order, that the intelligence community had failed in its analysis—creating one of the worst intelligence failures in U.S. history. He wrote:

"Most people in public life have passed through a defining experience they'd prefer to forget, and to be forgotten, but [it] won't be. So what can you do about it? How do you carry the burden?

"Everyone remembers my U.N. presentation. It had enormous impact and influence in this country and worldwide. It convinced many people that we were on the right course. Members of Congress told me that I had persuaded them to vote for a resolution supporting the President—even though they had voted for that resolution three months before I spoke to the U.N. My presentation became the case against Iraq. Who remembers any other?

"Yet seldom is it mentioned that every senior U.S. official would have made the exact same case, or that many of them were in fact making that case on television and in other public appearances. We had all been convinced by the same evidence. None of us knew that much of the evidence was wrong.

"If we had known there were no WMDs, there would have been no war."

For the rest of his life, General Powell was frequently asked about that famous U.N. speech. Although there was nothing he could do to change anything about it, he knew to follow his own well-known guidance, *"As always, drive through life looking through the front windshield and not the rearview mirror."*

And each year on February 5th, I reminded him that though sorrow followed, I was ever grateful he was able to share in my joy that first week of February 2003. In his book, *It Worked for Me*, he wrote, "A life is about its events; it's about challenges met and overcome—or not— it's about how we touch and are touched by the people we meet" (p. 279).

16.

The Last Chapter:
Mourning and One Final Gift

*"A mirror reflects a man's face, but what he is really
like is shown by the kind of friends he chooses."*
—Colin L. Powell

The Powell family summer vacation usually coincided with the annual forum of my Protocol & Diplomacy International–Protocol Officers Association (PDI-POA). The General was always supportive of my participation and leadership in this professional association and often acted as a sounding board and cheerleader whenever I sought his guidance. He enjoyed teasing me about my proper protocol ways, but I never doubted he was proud of my efforts.

In 2016, the PDI-POA annual forum was held in Atlanta. While the Powells were relaxing with dear friends on Long Island, I was enjoying time with my international protocol friends in Georgia.

Summer days in Atlanta are generally hot and humid and Wednesday, August 3, 2016 was exceptionally so. That morning we were assembled at Ebenezer Baptist Church, where Dr. Martin Luther King, Jr. had been co-pastor from 1960 until his assassination in 1968, and where his funeral had taken place. The church is in the historic area of downtown Atlanta designated as the Martin Luther King, Jr. National Historical Park, and we started the morning with a guided tour of the sanctuary provided by a historian. Afterwards we descended to the church's fellowship hall for our plenary session, which involved a panel discussion on official and state funerals called, "Ashes to Ashes, Dust to Dust: Meshing the Rituals of Death with the Demands of Protocol."

Ebenezer's fellowship hall, with its movable chairs and damp, air-conditioned coolness, felt just like so many other church fellowship halls I had been in throughout my life. It was the perfect setting for the session.

Towards the end of the panel discussion, I received a text message from General Powell. When I answered, I reminded him where I was and the significance of the location and discussion.

He responded, "*Little Bird, you do know you will be doing that for me someday, don't you?*"

When I read his message, I felt the blood drain from my face as my breath caught and my eyes teared, and I shivered in the chill of the air-conditioning. No longer able to focus on the panelists, I sent a reply that although I wasn't completely surprised by his message, his text was sobering. He answered we would talk about it in detail later but, when the time came, we would use Gawler's Sons Funeral Home, we would not choose his St. John's Episcopal Church in McLean for the service (too small), nor the Washington National Cathedral (too big and too important), and that he would be buried at Arlington National Cemetery, "*but down with the troops, not near the Eternal Flame or Tomb of the Unknown Soldier.*"

As I read his texts, I could barely breathe. Shock, fear, and sadness all competed for dominance in my mind.

When the plenary session ended, my friend Chris Young, former PDI-POA president and moderator of the plenary session, quickly approached me in the back of the room, as he'd noticed my reactions from the stage. Sonia Garza-Monarchi, another former PDI president, also gathered close. As I shared the text, still not able to speak, they both teared up. General Powell was dear to me personally, and to them he was a beloved leader they admired. The thought of his death sobered us all.

In the years that followed that text exchange, General Powell and I never had that follow-up conversation. I told myself that that inevitable day was surely still too far off in the future to worry about preparing for yet.

During our time together, I grew to appreciate how the General prided himself in taking good care of his health. He used the stationary bike in his basement daily and boasted he could still fit into his old army uniforms. The way he carried his six-foot-one frame made him a powerful presence wherever he went.

As reported in the press, General Powell had been treated for multiple myeloma for over a year prior to his death as well as for a more recently diagnosed Parkinson's disease. He and all of us close to him received the COVID-19 vaccines and boosters as soon as we could. Even so, he was the perfect example of how vulnerable an immunocompromised person is to the scourge of COVID-19.

On Wednesday, October 6, 2021, I joined the General in "the Bunker," his home office in the basement, to go over our various to-do lists, but mostly for me to see him and say goodbye before leaving town. The son of dear college friends Linda and Kord Basnight was getting married the following week in Williamsburg, Virginia, and I was the wedding coordinator—or "boss lady," as the wedding party affectionately dubbed me. As always, whenever

General Powell or I were to be out of town—even though we could always communicate wherever we were— we always planned an in-person chance to say a goodbye, safe travels, and hurry back before leaving.

With our usual kidding amidst our down-to-business moments, we spent normal—though in hindsight, precious—time together. He wished me well— knowing how much I enjoy being on the planning side of events and that I am like a kid in a candy store when helping with friends' weddings.

As always, he threw in a, "I'll miss you, so hurry back," before he hugged and kissed me goodbye.

At the time he was battling what we thought was only a cold. Unfortunately, the cold symptoms continued to get worse over the following days.

Our talks on the phone multiple times daily were interspersed with our typical WhatsApp messages—me reporting on the joy of wedding arrangements, him sharing the gossip and news from the Bunker as well as acknowledging that his cold symptoms were pretty bad and not getting better.

On Monday, October 11th, he tested positive for COVID-19 and was rushed by ambulance to Walter Reed National Military Medical Center to be admitted to the ICU.

Despite restrictions forbidding cellphones in the ICU, few servicemen or women would likely deny a former Joint Chief Chairman's request to have one. So two days later, when my phone vibrated in my pocket during a pre-wedding cocktail party, I tucked myself into a garden corner, relieved to hear his voice. He teased and scolded me, telling me not to be too much of a drill sergeant ordering around the wedding attendants. He said that although he'd hoped to be home on Saturday, the doctors were talking about keeping him through the weekend, so I teased him to please follow the doctors' orders. I also passed along that his friend, former Secretary of State Madeleine Albright, had called me earlier that day to ask how he was and to pass along her love.

Although I could hear the noises associated with hospitals and ventilators, the joy of hearing his voice and sharing a laugh was an incredible relief. Like the surrogate dad he was to me, not for the first time we closed the conversation by saying "*I love you*" to each other.

I'm sure his family members and closest friends have similar stories of precious phone calls from the ICU. Doubtless they experienced these as a remarkable final blessing as well.

Although the next three days were filled with joyful wedding celebrations, part of my heart remained troubled. And then, before dawn Monday morning, I received the heartbreaking news from Michael Powell: his dad had passed just minutes before.

I was devastated. The mentor, friend, and leader I had served with so much joy was gone. I will never meet his equal. I will not pretend to speak for the heartbreak that Mrs. Powell, the children, and grandchildren experienced, nor for that of any of the General's other loved ones, but my grief was almost paralyzing. Theirs surely must have been even more so.

I was still in Williamsburg, having planned to leave for Northern Virginia that day around noon, so I needed the Powell family to decide if it would be better for me to stay there by the phone for a while or get on the road and be incommunicado for the two-and-a-half-hour drive home. One of the daughters responded immediately, "*Mom says she needs you here.*"

It was barely daybreak but there were calls I had to make before heading north. I called my family and could barely say the words before adding a plea for strength. Outside my family, there were two others who I knew should hear the news from me rather than from the news release that would be breaking shortly.

First, I called Washington Speakers Bureau co-founder Harry Rhoads, as the General still had a couple speaking engagements scheduled for the next few weeks. I knew once the story broke Harry would be inundated with calls from clients and other speakers.

I then called Madeleine Albright. I had gotten to know her quite well during the many events she and General Powell had shared. I had also called her the day he entered the hospital and, as I mentioned earlier, she had called me for status reports during the week after. This time, as heartbreaking as the news was for her to hear, Dr. Albright extended to me compassionate words of support: "*Leslie, you have my love.*"

My drive seemed interminable, yet I arrived home in record time. My mother consoled me while providing updates and one thing became increasingly clear: there were angels among us who would be helping us through our grief. One of these angels was Mrs. Powell's dear friend Jan Smith who had already called my home twice. Jan passed along encouragement but also, as a member of Washington National Cathedral, she shared contact information in case the family wanted the funeral there.

Nearly everyone has experienced the loss of a close friend or loved one, and even those who haven't yet must eventually accept it as inevitable. Having worked over thirty years in protocol, I am well versed in organizing official funerals and memorial ceremonies and have even given speeches on the topic to international audiences. For the first time though, I was going to help plan a funeral for a world leader while simultaneously mourning one of my closest and dearest friends.

In the Old Testament, the third chapter of Ecclesiastes reminds us that for everything there is a season. Its fourth verse asserts that there is "*a time to weep, and a time to laugh; a time to mourn, and a time to dance*" (King James Version).

I had danced at the wedding, just days before the General's death. Now it was time to weep.

There is no way to adequately recognize all the many people—friends and family members, friends of friends, and kind and gifted public servants behind the scenes—who made the eighteen days between General Powell's death and his funeral survivable. Even so, I will share some of the gentle moments of grace these angels on earth showed us as reminders that the smallest kindness can be a welcome balm in moments of sorrow. Each of us can make a difference to someone experiencing grief with just the right touch at just the right time.

By the time I arrived at the Powell residence in McLean, Mrs. Powell had designated the little library to the left of the front door as my "office," and from there I would manage the calls and gestures of condolence that continuously arrived. The dining room table directly across the entryway from me was command central, where we would coordinate the funeral and burial. As always, General Powell's Principal Assistant, Peggy Cifrino, masterfully handled the press among so many other things from there. As it was during the General's life, Peggy and I would be part of the extended family in the trying days ahead.

Despite that text conversation General Powell and I had all those years ago, the family believed the National Cathedral should be used for the funeral service if available. I reached out to Jan Smith's recommended contact—the cathedral's Provost, The Reverend Canon Jan Cope. During the call, Reverend

Cope shared with me that the cathedral leadership had been standing by from the moment they heard the news. They had not assumed anything but had wanted to be prepared in case the family called.

After many conversations with various cathedral officials, the funeral was scheduled for Friday, the 5th of November, and we began tackling the myriad details and decisions necessary for the service. Because we were all still in the grip of the pandemic, we kept the guest list limited to stay well within the restricted COVID-19 spacing the cathedral required. Guests were "by invitation only," and everyone had to be masked and vaccinated. An outside contractor was hired to manage the invitation process and we began seeking and confirming contact information for the invitees.

The endless hours of funeral planning were punctuated almost nonstop by the sound of phones ringing with condolence calls from all over the world, the arrival of the post office's daily delivery of bags of cards and letters, and the chime of the doorbell alerting us to another thoughtful gift of food or flowers. While juggling the planning calls and meetings with the funeral home, cemetery, cathedral, Department of Defense, and the U.S. Secret Service, we spent every moment possible updating the contact information of the guests invited to the memorial service, an important reminder we should always keep our contact lists current for such times.

My dear friends and longtime protocol colleagues, Larry Dunham, former Assistant Chief of Protocol for Diplomatic Affairs, and April Guice, former deputy Assistant Chief of Protocol for Ceremonials, answered my call to build and manage a protocol team that would be on duty at the cathedral throughout the funeral. As I would be seated with the family for the service, turning this responsibility over to these dear friends, knowing they would ask for the best-of-the-best among our colleagues, was a tremendous comfort.

The gifted public servants whom Larry and April recruited were all experts and friends. They spent hours doing advance work with officials from the White House, State Department, and the cathedral's gifted Director of Guest and Event Management Services, Valerie Ciccone. After vigorous discussion, they designed the complicated seating charts, following the strict protocol required for the limited officials who would be assigned seats in the front of the cathedral. They then instructed the cathedral volunteers on how to get those guests to the right place on the day of the service.

The President and each of the attending former presidents and first ladies would arrive in separate motorcades at a restricted cathedral entrance, so the team did their best to placate guests inconvenienced by the requisite security arrangements. Not only did all guests have to be masked and vaccinated, they had to come early to go through "mags" (i.e., magnetometers) before entering the cathedral. All these requirements meant the process would be frustrating for many and the team would have to be ready to deal with any issues on the spot with polished tact.

Fortunately, the cathedral staff took care of all the arrangements for the seating and the positioning of the media both inside and outside the cathedral.

General Powell's funeral would not be a state funeral, as the only ones eligible for a state funeral are chiefs of state, so we were not obligated to include all members of Congress nor the full diplomatic corps on the guest list. The family decided this funeral would be private and personal, inviting only those with whom they had personal relationships. Current and former Department of State and Defense officials would be invited and have assigned seats, but only a handful of personal friends from Congress were included.

Likewise, aside from the few ambassadors with whom the General was friends, only the regional deans (that is, the senior ranking ambassador of each of the six diplomatic regions of the world) would be invited.

Among the many angels on staff at the cathedral, I am forever indebted to The Reverend Canon Rose Duncan, Canon for Worship. After numerous phone conversations, when I finally met her upon arriving for the first cathedral walk through, she hugged me. When my tears started and I tried to pull away, she held on tighter, sternly admonishing me, "Don't you pull away! I'm not finished hugging you." I am not sure there were any words or gestures I needed more in that moment. Even today, that memory of her loving acceptance of my grief is comforting.

Late one night after coming home from the Powell residence, I listened to a voicemail from William "Buddy" Carter. Buddy was the first friend I ever made in protocol over three decades ago. He had retired just months before as White House butler after serving for 47 years across ten presidential administrations. *"Leslie, this is Buddy, just calling to check on you, darling. Didn't want anything in particular. Love you."* Hearing his message was another reminder that the words and gestures we give to others when they are grieving can be lifelines.

Condolences came in from all over the world. From friends and loved ones of course, but also notes from strangers wanting to share how much the General meant to them. Unless the handwriting on the note and the return address were illegible, Mrs. Powell sent a note of thanks in response to each person for months after the funeral.

Many, many years before, General Powell was keynote speaker at an event for a funeral home conglomerate. Although I no longer remember the company's name, I do remember how much the General enjoyed his time with the leadership—so much that they invited him to join their board of directors. He declined, but I will always remember him telling me how each official with whom he interacted had a special presence.

That was certainly true of my—*our*—contact with Gawler's Sons Funeral Home. As the General had instructed in our original text conversation, Gawler's was the funeral home we used. Josh Carter could not have been a better servant leader and I am honored to consider him now a friend. With grace and efficiency, he handled every painful task required for a family preparing for a funeral. In the final couple days before the service, Josh arranged for Frank Branch and Eric Holmes, former military men and beloved past and current members of the Powell household staff, to come to the funeral home to inspect the General's uniform so it would be as perfect as possible in both life and in death.

It was also a blessing to work with Mike Wagner, Chief of National Events Planning for the Military District of Washington, as he was involved in all the movements at the cathedral and cemetery. With the General being buried at Arlington National Cemetery, and the President of the United States as well as former presidents attending the service at the cathedral, there would be extraordinary security requirements every step of the way. Mike and I spoke a common language of protocol, but with a sensitivity beyond what was demanded of the job, Mike walked me through every moment of our movements with kindness and grace.

Since General Powell was to be buried immediately after the service, getting the family and extended family from the Cathedral to the cemetery was a logistical challenge. I had confirmed with Josh and the team at the funeral home that in addition to the car for the immediate family, we would have five mini-buses transporting the extended family from McLean to the cathedral, to the cemetery, and finally back to McLean. This required the motorcade to make a roundtrip through three different police jurisdictions: Fairfax County, the National Park Service, and Washington, D.C. Mike provided professional guidance throughout the many days of planning, and gentle encouragement while I was seated beside him in the lead car ahead of the hearse in the funeral procession.

Just before I got into our car the morning of the funeral, I checked my email and found a message from a member of my own church's clergy. The Old Presbyterian Meeting House associate pastor, Katherine Stanford, wrote simply, *"I'm thinking of you and sending up prayers on this difficult day as you mourn your dear friend, especially having had to plan and work hard to create this day to honor him. I join you and the world in sadness grieving Gen. Powell. Take good care of yourself, especially in the days to come."* This message, the balm I needed at that moment, was a poignant reminder that many people around the world were grieving, too.

No doubt every funeral procession seems both interminable and over too fast. The morning was bright and sunny, though cold. From my vantage point in the motorcade, I felt as though I were in a dream as I watched the police escort on so many motorcycles with flashing lights lead us down the George Washington Memorial Parkway, out of Virginia, and over the Potomac River into D.C. It was also surreal to see people gathered in the cold on street corners—some with cameras, some just standing out of respect or maybe even just curiosity—as our funeral motorcade pulled slowly into the circle drive in front of the cathedral steps.

As soon as we arrived, the extended family members were escorted to their seats and the immediate family was led into the holding room just inside the front doors to the right. I was to be seated in the family section next to Marybel Batjer—one of the General's very best friends— who would be doing one of the readings in the service; but I was to stay with the family in the hold room for a few minutes first, in order to introduce them to the cathedral leadership. Over the past many days, I had spoken with and met most of the clergy in person, but the family was now meeting them for the first time.

At the appropriate time, Mike Wagner cued me that it was time to leave the family and be seated. Holding onto the arm of a military escort while walking down the long center aisle to my seat was a gift, the strong arm serving as a steadying anchor. As I made my way forward, I remembered the words my dear friend and member of the protocol team, Bunny Murdock, had texted me the night before, "*You got this! Shoulders back, chin up—make him proud!*"

There is a moment in the PBS coverage that shows me (unidentified) on the arm of my escort straightening my shoulders and putting my chin up at the exact moment I recalled Bunny's inimitable words.

Everything at the cathedral operated like clockwork thanks to the extraordinary skill of the cathedral clergy and staff. The team of beloved protocol colleagues performed flawlessly and, working with the cathedral volunteers, made sure all guests were well cared for.

The service was as we all had wanted and hoped. For those who did not hear the words and the music of the service live, I rejoice we can listen again through numerous internet recordings.

Hearing Wintley Phipps singing the hymn "How Great Thou Art" at the front of the cathedral is breathtaking, and each of the readings is a message that needs to be heard again and again.

General Powell had many dear friends, but without doubt, as well as having been his Deputy at the State Department, Richard "Rich" Armitage was his best friend and had been for decades. Rich shared several heartwarming anecdotes, providing the audience much needed comic relief. In one, he described Secretary Powell getting down on one knee in front of visiting Foreign Minister of Sweden Ann Linde to sing the song "Mamma Mia" after receiving her gift of ABBA's greatest hits on CD.

Madeleine Albright's eulogy for her longtime friend ended with a beautiful charge for us all:

> This morning, my heart aches because we have lost a friend, and our nation one of its finest and most loyal soldiers. Yet even as we contemplate the magnitude of our loss, we can almost hear a familiar voice asking us, no—commanding us—to stop feeling sad, to turn our gaze once again from the past to the future, and to get on with the nation's business, while making the absolute most of our own days on earth.

However, no words in that service could resonate more though than those of Michael Powell. Speaking on behalf of the family, the General's beloved son admonished, "The example of Colin Powell does not call on us to emulate his resume, which is too formidable for mere mortals. It is to emulate his character and his example as a human being. We can strive to do that. We can choose to be good."

And no matter how many tears I have shed while rewatching

clips of the funeral and hearing the tributes, it's impossible not to smile when hearing the military musicians perfectly and joyfully play Bob Marley's "Three Little Birds" and ABBA's "Dancing Queen" at the beginning of the service, beautifully expressing the *joie de vivre* that characterized so many aspects of General Powell's remarkable life.

At the end of the funeral service, we proceeded down that long center aisle, following the casket back to the motorcade. The formal service that was shared with the world was now over. I mentioned in the beginning of the book that lives of service can make the world a better place. As we walked out of the cathedral, I knew we had celebrated the life of someone who had done just that and I found the words from Matthew 25:21 resonating in my mind:

"Well done, good and faithful servant" (King James Version).

Our ride to Arlington National Cemetery passed in thoughtful silence, then suddenly we were graveside and faced with the hundreds of service men and women standing in formation for the burial of one of our military's highest-ranking officers. As General Powell had wished, he would rest "down with the troops."

It was late afternoon now, so at certain angles the setting sun was blinding. Shielding my eyes at General Powell's grave site, I was overwhelmed with the contrasting memories of standing in pouring rain at my father's burial as a little girl.

Once many, many years ago, General Powell had asked me to say his name, and although I knew he was giving me permission to call him Colin, I responded with a smile saying, "Which one?" then proceeded to rattle off any of a number of official as well as cheeky ones: General Powell, *the* General, CP, GP, Uncle Gen, Bro P, even Colin-Baby (as a reporter friend of his called him),

Poppy (as he was known within the family), and Sir. With a laugh, he gave up and didn't press it or mention it again.

Nevertheless, he understood I knew he was giving me permission to use his first name. And I knew he understood that no matter how close we were, I would always give him a quiet deference for all he represented and had accomplished.

One of the General's favorite singers was the Scottish singer Lulu, who made famous the song "To Sir With Love," which was written by Don Black and Mark London for the movie of that same name starring Sidney Portier. Although the lyrics of the song are written as if sung by a young schoolgirl adoringly to her teacher, my eyes tear whenever I think of the last verse:

A friend who taught right from wrong
And weak from strong
That's a lot to learn,
What, what can I give you in return?
If you wanted the moon
I would try to make a start
But I would rather you
Let me give my heart
To Sir with love.

By the time I fell into General Powell's world over a quarter century ago, I had long known right from wrong. And yet, by the way he lived his life, the example he set, he showed us all right from wrong, weak from strong, and so much more. If I could have given him the moon to go with his four stars, I surely would have.

As a military leader and later as a senior statesman on the world stage, he had our admiration and respect.

As a boss, a dear friend, and a surrogate father, he had my heart and I will forever rejoice in being able to share the gift of his memory, his lessons, and his *joie de vivre*.

To Sir with love.
Indeed.

ACKNOWLEDGEMENTS

With this book, I have a new appreciation for an author's opportunity to express heartfelt gratitude. Although I may have skipped over the acknowledgements section in many books I have read in the past, I now promise to read every one going forward in hopes that every reader of mine will read this one and know that each person I mention by name is someone whose name I want to shout from the rooftops with either my gratitude, respect, love, admiration, or a combination of all four.

My mother and brother—Margaret Lautenslager and Edwin "Win" Lautenslager—are and always will be my biggest cheerleaders as well as loving critics. I can only wish everyone were so blessed to have their support and love. What most readers of this book will not realize is that they are both pretty incredible editors as well. Go read General Powell's acknowledgements in *It Worked For Me* if you have any doubts.

I believe in serendipity and Santa Claus! It is through both that I came to know, admire, and respect my collaborator, Bradley Harper; my literary agent and publisher, Lisa Hagan; and my editor, Petra Winters. In November 2022, I was having dinner in Williamsburg, Virginia with my dear friend Linda Basnight, who was to leave me there for a few days of solitude devoted to beginning this book. Because our original dinner plans fell through, we ended up seated outside under heat lamps at a little French restaurant called Le Yaca. Shortly after we ordered, a lovely couple—Chere and Brad Harper—sat down at the table beside ours and started a conversation. Over the course of that dinner, we learned Brad was a retired Army colonel and doctor of pathology, and that he and his wife shared mutual friends with Linda's parents (her dad being a retired Army brigadier general); Brad had been stationed in Italy during Desert Storm and while there had to keep on hand an appropriate blood supply for the then Chairman of the Joint Chiefs (i.e., General Powell). To top it all off, in retirement Brad was—in fact—Busch Garden's Santa Claus.

When we learned Brad was also an accomplished and award-winning author, Linda pointed to me and exclaimed, "My friend won't tell you this but I will—she's writing a book, too!" From that serendipitous meeting, a wonderful partnership was born. Knowing that General Powell had a collaborator for both of his books, I readily accepted Brad's willingness to be mine. He has provided wordsmithing expertise, critical guidance, and unwavering support. I am truly thankful he insisted that I write the last chapter right away, knowing it would be painful but also knowing it would make everything that followed all the easier. Through a friend of Brad's, we were introduced to Lisa Hagan and I will forever be grateful she was willing to gamble on this unknown author within just a day of our initial phone call. The icing on the cake to connecting with Lisa was the serendipitous discovery that she had attended high school with cousins of mine in Richmond and we each had a grandmother renowned and beloved within the Miller & Rhodes community of old. It truly is a delightfully small world. Brad also connected me with Petra Winters, a truly remarkable editor. With her deft and yet gentle figurative red pen alerting me to what I didn't know that I didn't know about the mechanics of writing, she has provided an invaluable polish to my manuscript and I will forever sing her praises. I am also very grateful to my friend Clay Doherty, who generously shared his PR and communications skills with gentle though persistent guidance on how to best launch this story out into the world.

Knowing I had enthusiastic support from General Powell's two best friends, Marybel Batjer and Rich Armitage, to even attempt this book leaves me almost at a loss for words. I adore them both and count myself lucky that my General brought them into my life.

I will forever be beholden to Ambassador Selwa "Lucky" Roosevelt. She, of course, is the one who first introduced me to the world of protocol without which I would never have had the opportunity to fall into the General's world. In addition, she shared her considerable talents as an accomplished author herself, providing invaluable and critical guidance on how to be a better writer.

For the team of protocol professionals tapped to work miracles the day of General Powell's funeral, there are not sufficient words to describe my gratitude for the generous gifts of their time and professional expertise, not to mention their loving friendship. To Larry Dunham, April Guice, Bunny Murdock, Mary Claire Murphy, Steve Boley, Richard Rogers, Daphne Martinez, Jessie Johnson, Penny Price, Tanya Turner, Chenobia Calhoun, Jennifer Nicholson, Sandy Carnes Alvarez, Aracelli Fullem, Mauri Earl, David Nelson, Laura Wills, Laura Parker, Diane Robertson, Carolina Bonina, Janet Eissenstat, Pooneh Butler, Sarah Farnsworth, and Kristina Jeter, I thank you. And to anyone reading this, know that if you are ever lucky enough to meet or know anyone from this group of beloved colleagues and friends, you are blessed.

To the many friends cheering me along throughout this writing adventure, thank you. I questioned my ability to see this through on many occasions, wondering who am I to try and appropriately paint this picture of the Colin Powell I knew. To Linda and Kord Basnight, Lanie Denslow, Lisa Fikes, Lisa Walker Hart, Elisa Gambino Broffman, Linda Halstead, Barbara Pope, Caroline Korte, Ross Harding, Kari Michaelson, the FOLD,

Kim Townsend, Graciela Rivas, Debi Schiff, Maggie Jones, Babs Chase, Kim Starfield, PDI-POA friends around the world, 3rd floor Barrett babes, W&M Kappas of the '80s at our centennial celebration, Amy Parsons, the MacLeod family, Helen Cox, Michele Woodward, Chris Keppler, Timmy Sullivan, Mike Salmon, Anne Pallotta, and so many more—you have all provided tremendous encouragement throughout these many months and I am truly in your debt. Thank you, dear friends. Your kind words at just the right moments made a difference.

And to Mrs. Powell, Michael and Jane, Linda, Anne and Francis, and all the grandkids, thank you for sharing your beloved Poppy with the world and with me.

Leslie Lautenslager's career in protocol began in 1986 when she was hired by U.S. Chief of Protocol Selwa "Lucky" Roosevelt as assistant to the manager of Blair House, the President's Guest House. Ambassador Roosevelt later promoted her to a protocol officer in the Ceremonials and then Visits division at the U.S. State Department. In addition to working on state and official visits of chiefs of state and heads of government, she organized and lead delegations representing President Reagan at various events around the world. After her administration appointment ended, Leslie joined the Battle of Normandy Foundation where she oversaw special events and protocol for over five years leading up to the 50th anniversary of D-Day.

Her life changed in April 1996 when she was hired by the co-founders of the Washington Speakers Bureau to assist one of the most popular speakers on the international stage: General Colin L. Powell, USA (Ret.). Despite their different backgrounds, they quickly developed a unique rapport and language that lasted until his death over 25 years later. On the professional speaking circuit, she was his liaison to clients, responsible for the logistical details of travel and preparations to make him "smart" about each event.

When General Powell was confirmed as the U.S. Secretary of State, she served as the Assistant Chief of Protocol for Ceremonials and Special Assistant to the Secretary of State, responsible for a staff tasked with planning and organizing all functions hosted by the Secretary to honor foreign dignitaries. Additionally, she supported ceremonies on behalf of the President and Vice President for national commemorations, the annual opening of the United Nations General Assembly, and state funerals, among many others. In 2005 after the General's four-year tenure as the world's top diplomat, she returned with him to the speaking circuit.

A graduate of the College of William & Mary, she has a Bachelor of Arts degree with a double major in Psychology and in Fine Arts.

Bradley Harper is a retired US Army COL and pathologist who, after a brief and undistinguished stint as an Infantry officer went to medical school. He retired after thirty-seven years of active duty with four commands and two years in the Pentagon on the personal staff of the US Army Surgeon General. His writing credits include *A Knife in the Fog*, a 2019 Edgars Finalist in which a young Arthur Conan Doyle stalks Jack the Ripper. COL Harper has an associate degree in creative writing from Full Sail University, and a Masters in Creative Writing from Napier University in Edinburgh, Scotland.

Brad recently directed and produced an animation adaptation of a poem he composed called "Dark Tryst," which won Best Super Short Film at the January 2023 Paris Film Awards.

www.BHarperAuthor.Com